Contents

DANCE, NANI, DANCE

STORIES OF GRANDMOTHERS AND GRANDFATHERS

FOREWORD BY RUSKIN BOND

EDITED WITH AN INTRODUCTION BY

BULBUL SHARMA

talking CUB
An Imprint of Speaking Tiger Books

TALKING CUB
Published by Speaking Tiger Books LLP
125A, Ground Floor, Shahpur Jat,
Near Asiad Village, New Delhi - 110 049

Published in Talking Cub by Speaking Tiger Books in paperback in 2023

ISBN: 978-93-5447-481-1
eISBN: 978-93-5447-488-0

10 9 8 7 6 5 4 3 2 1

Typeset in Lora by Jojy Philip
Printed at HT Media Ltd, Greater Noida

Bulbul Sharma is an artist and author. She has written more than twenty books, both for children and adults. She spends a lot of time in the mountains birdwatching. She has five grandchildren—Naina, Shivam, Samara, Prithvi and Shiv.

Foreword

When I was six years old, and Granny was sixty, she tried teaching me to waltz. She was large and bulky, and I was very small. We cavorted around her small sitting-room to the strains of 'The Blue Danube', played on an old wind-up gramophone. Outside the bungalow was our River Danube—in the form of a small irrigation canal, flowing swiftly down to the dhobi ghats. Initially, our waltz ended up on the floor, as we knocked over Granny's bridge table. Viennese waltz needs space, after all. But we got better at it.

The bungalow and the canal have long since disappeared, making way for more people and more high-rise buildings. But I still have photographs of Granny, and I can listen to 'The Blue Danube' any time I want now, thanks to the

YouTube on my granddaughter Shrishti's app (or whatever it's called).

My Granny was really a stern, no-nonsense person, best remembered for her Kitchen Proverbs. These went something like: 'Don't let your tongue cut your throat' (this was for when I ate too much); 'better a small fish than an empty dish' (if I complained that there wasn't enough); and 'there is skill in all things, even in making porridge'.

Although at times I was a troublesome boy, Granny must have been quite fond of me, for it was the small insurance policy that she took out in my name that was to enable me to go abroad when I had finished school. It was while I was living in England for a few years, that my first book *The Room on the Roof* was accepted by a publisher. So in some way Granny was responsible for my being a published writer too.

Granny spent her last years in Ranchi, and her grave still carries a brief epitaph beneath her name Ellen Clerke, placed there by her three daughters: 'She did her best for all of us'.

I think that says it all.

I hope this book of grandparents will help all of us, whether young or old, to think of our grandparents. And if some of us are lucky enough, to spend some extra time with them, sharing some music, or a story, or even a song on an app.

Ruskin Bond

Introduction

Grandparents always adore their grand-children, however naughty or badly behaved they are; even if they never win a prize at sports or in their studies. Only your grandfather or your grandmother will find something lovable about that pimple on your nose or that smudge on your fingertips. My mother would scold me when I got poor marks in my exams but my grandmother would tell me, 'Ask her what good marks *she* got for making paper flowers.'

Your father will be very annoyed if you break the neighbour's windowpane but you know what your grandfather will say? 'It was not his fault. The glass was cracked in any case, waiting to be broken.'

Your grandparents love you and think you are perfect in every way. And I am sure, you also think that your grandparents are just fantastic.

In some of the stories you will read in this book, children find different ways to show how much they love their grandparents. Some kids are a bit shy or hesitant at first when they meet their grandparents after many years, and others are slightly baffled by the things old people often do.

Bijal Vachharajani's story 'My Grandma Hoards Stuff', is about a grandmother who was an intrepid traveller, who defied the US Immigration officials with bravado and almost managed to sneak a bottle of mango pickle into the US. Then in Ashok Rajagopalan's story we meet a duo of very clever detective-grandparents who solve a tricky case of the Poster Prankster.

Many of us, both grown-ups and children, have sad but fond memories of our grandparents when they are no longer with us. We often remember the food they cooked for us or recall some special toy they made for us with their own hands. Ruskin Bond paints a very unusual picture and takes us back to a day in the life of his beloved grandmother when she was a bold, feisty young girl. This charming story will make you smile as all Ruskin Bond stories do.

My story is about my Dida who was very fond of solving mysteries and often a bit too inquisitive about other people's business. But she was great fun to travel with. Swapna Dutta's Dadu had a very unusual pet—a tiger! She tells us about how the tiger grew from a baby cub to full-grown animal in their grandfather's house. Sadly, they had to part one day.

Many of you must have spent time in your grandparents' house during the long summer holidays. I remember a wild garden with a stream running through my Dida's house and lots of lovely places to play hide and seek. In 'A Typical Vacation' by Nandini Nayar we meet two children getting very bored since there is no Wi-Fi and no mobile phones in their grandparents' house and worse still, their grandparents are very distant and aloof. Gradually Sarika and Sachin forget their phones and find out new ways of looking at things. They also get to know their grandparents and learn to share lots of wonderful new things with them.

Suddenly things begin to look very exciting in 'Dance, Nani, Dance!' by Deepa Agarwal. In this heartbreaking yet delightful story we see how a granddaughter's perception about old ladies changes when she discovers her Nani loves to dance and that she dances really well. But there is a wistful twist to the tale too.

We all love mysteries and if there is a ghost thrown in, then so much the better. 'Something Fishy in the Neighbourhood' by Sayantan Ghosh has both. Here we meet a scaly, slimy ghost with red eyes who loves fish curry. This enjoyable story is set in a decrepit old haunted house—my favourite setting for a story! In the story, Sunny and his clever Dadu finally solve the mystery and everyone is happy, including the scaly creature.

When our grandparents pass away, we are filled with deep sadness and it seems we will never recover from this loss. Ashok Banker's beautifully written story is about loss. A young boy, very gifted and sensitive, somehow manages to communicate with his beloved Nani, who is no longer in this world.

In 'Where Peacocks Dance' by Adithi Rao, we meet a young girl who wants to become a master craftsman like her grandfather and embroider zardozi motifs—and then magic happens in the moonlight.

Secrets are shared between a granddaughter and her grandmother in Varsha Seshan's story 'Hide and Seek' and a few delicious Diwali treats are added to make the tale tastier.

We look at some serious issues in 'My Grandmother and Her Daughter' by Harshikaa Udasi. It is a poignant story set in the turbulent period during Partition and then the story moves to 1993 when communal riots took place in Mumbai. A lost child is taken home safely by a grandmother who had lost her own daughter many years ago.

Which child can resist a story about a locked room where you are not allowed in? 'The Forbidden Room' by Andaleeb Wajid tells us about such a room where Maya's strict grandfather has hidden a delightful surprise.

Nandu has to deal with a lively grandmother who calls herself a 'soulful apparition' and though she has passed on, she now suddenly appears dressed in torn jeans and magenta-streaked hair! It is a charming and funny tale by Menaka Raman.

'The Surprise Act' by Nandita da Cunha is a heartwarming story about a grandfather discovering many new things thanks to the Grandparents Day in school!

Jerry Pinto will make you smile and shed a quiet tear in his story 'When Granny Died'. 'Is she a star or a tiny sliver of stardust? Is she a moth or a butterfly?' wonders a young boy as he tries to deal with his grandmother's death.

All the stories in this book will make you think about your grandparents and if you are lucky enough to have them with you, perhaps you can read this book together and have lots of fun.

We will always remember our grandparents with joy however old we get. They are a link to our happy childhood days, they are the mountain peak, the bubbling spring from where we have launched ourselves into our life's journey ahead.

Bulbul Sharma

Proud grandmother of 5!

My Grandma Hoards Stuff

BIJAL VACHHARAJANI

Yes, there is a single-use plastic ban across the world.

Finally.

It was long overdue.

We were drowning in plastic. Bags for fruits. Bags for vegetables. Bags for bags. Double bagging cold drinks. Bags for one item. Bags for sixty-five items.

Now everyone had to carry their own cloth bag, or pay for one.

Everyone except Dadi.

The thing is, my grandma hoards stuff.

She keeps everything for eons, seventy whole eons and a half.

She has sachets of shampoos, the ones that came as samples in newspaper ads. They had to be torn and used. She would remove them and neatly put them in a Tupperware dabba whose lid had accidently melted a bit when kept on top of a steaming milk pan. Sachets of detergent samples. Sachets of perfumed bags. Empty cloth sachets to put money or gifts in.

Dadi had also kept all the transistor radios, gramophones, cassette players, CD players, cassettes, LPs, CDs that she had been gifted by our extremely large family. None of them worked anymore, but she refused to throw them out. 'You never know when you need them,' she would tell us. Papa kept trying to sneak out her LPs but she would snap at him, and he'd retreat.

Then she had a magnificent array of containers of all sizes, shapes and material, ranging from plastic to silicone to metal to you name it, she had it. They were stacked like Russian Matryoshka dolls, each one opened to reveal another, and another in its depths. If there was a museum of dabbas somewhere, she would have been named chief contributor and a sculpture of dabbas made in her honour. Right at the entrance.

I had once gone to a really fancy art gallery on a field trip, where we had seen an art installation made entirely out of steel utensils. People were taking photos and discussing it with big words. But all I could think was that my Dadi had way more steel utensils than this artist. He should come and make an installation with them. If she'd part with them, that is.

Back to the plastic ban. Everyone was rejoicing. Some were worrying. And my Dadi...

Well, my Dadi had prepared for this eventuality for the last seventy-five years. Okay, maybe not seventy-five, but at least since she was twenty, so that means fifty years. For half a century, she had been squirrelling away plastic bags of all colours, sizes and microns. They were compressed, folded, and stowed away carefully in...bigger plastic bags. It was like a stash of illegal rainbows.

We knew when the apocalypse came, Dadi would be prepared, one plastic bag, one sachet, one utensil, one transistor at a time.

Right now the bags were coming in handy as Dadi was off to the US of A. She was visiting her favouritest daughter, who lived there with her favouritest son-in-law and favouritest two grandsons. We were girls, we were way down the favouritest ladder.

Preparations had been going on for days. Snacks were made (and double bagged in plastic). Shopping was done. Suitcases were being packed, weighed, unpacked, repacked. Arguments ensued, about what could be taken and not taken.

A tornado full of suitcases had taken over our home, and everywhere my sister and I went, we tripped over one. We had to keep fishing Catrina out of the bags because she thought all of them were exclusively for her. So our jet black cat would climb on top of Aanchal Fui's hand-knitted bright red sweater and curl up to sleep. We would be able to locate her as grandma would shriek down the house. She hated black cats. 'Shoo, shoo, cat,' we would hear her yelling. Catrina would yawn and dig in her claws further, until one of us came and rescued her from Dadi.

But finally it was D-Day, or rather USA-Day. It was going to be a loooooong flight. New Delhi to Paris. Paris to Ohio. Many, many hours.

All her bags were packed, and Dadi was ready to go. Mummy was in the car, making space in the boot for Dadi's two ginormous suitcases, which could easily have fitted Rinki, Catrina and me, and left space enough for Chintan and Yogesh from my class. Rinki and I had to sit on top of the suitcases to get them to shut, that's how oozing with stuff they were.

Papa dragged the suitcases out, while we pretended to hold the other side and push. Catrina kept trying to trip us over, woebegone at the thought of her comfy suitcases leaving without her. Mummy honked twice, it was getting late, and of course there would be traffic.

Dadi trotted out. Her white hair was neatly combed into a bun, her crisp cotton sari was pinned up and pleated carefully, and her gold bangles were glinting in the sun. Her face was creased into a huge smile, as big as her load—one diaper bag (it has more room, she insisted), one purse with her passport and tickets, our second Fui's address, and a mobile phone. And three plastic bags.

'No, no, no,' Papa shook his head, and tried to grab the plastic bags from her. 'You can't take these on the flight, they won't allow you.'

Dadi stuck out her lower lip. When she did that, everyone knew she was stepping into her, 'I am your mother, you're my son, and not the other way round' phase. She did that when Papa said she can't put more ghee on her paratha, when she reached for a second helping of boondi laddoo, and when she insisted on a cold bath on a cold day (don't waste electricity, in my days...). That's when we saw Papa transform into a ten-year-old boy, who didn't know how to argue with his mother.

But this time, he was more worried about international customs than his mother's pouty face. He grabbed the three bags and began rifling through them.

Bag 1 had a comb, a bottle of hair oil inside another bag, and a sweater.

'You can't take hair oil, what if it spills,' Papa yelled. 'Plus only 100 ml liquids are allowed.'

The lip stuck out more. It was like watching Pinocchio lie. 'I need my hair oil, I make it myself. It has neem, ashwagandha, coconut oil, onion skin.' Dadi only spoke Gujarati, and understood Hindi but did not speak it.

Papa's face was looking like an onion skin now. 'No, they will confiscate it.'

'As if I'd let them.' All of four feet, seven inches Dadi drew up to her full height that made absolutely no difference.

'Do you want them to throw it away? Am sure Sandhya will make you some.' He firmly removed the oil and stowed the comb and sweater in the diaper bag, shaking his head.

Mummy honked again. Papa hurriedly inspected the second bag. It had a water bottle, a flask of milky, sugary coffee, a carton of juice, and lots of straws and forks and spoons. He didn't even bother asking her. He stuffed the water bottle and one spoon in the side pocket of the diaper bag and gave the other things to Rinki to put away. He did it so fast that Dadi had no time to protest. 'You can drink the coffee in the car.'

The third bag was opened, and it was a bagful of...puffed rice. Not just any puffed rice. Dadi would roast the puffed rice until they were crisp, and then toss them in hot ghee with salt, turmeric, hing, onions and peanuts.

Papa glowered at her. But before he could say anything, Dadi snatched the bag back, tied a top knot deftly sealing in her favourite snack and said, 'I am diabetic, I need to eat.'

'Yes, but we've informed the airline and there'll be plenty of suitable food...'

She turned to him and he immediately went quiet. 'I am travelling with the mumra, or not going AT ALL.'

'That's a bit excessive,' Rinki whispered to me. She loved using big words and showing off that she was older to me by four years, three months, sixteen days.

I gaped at her, 'What?'

'Arre, too much,' she said. Now she was shaking her head, looking just like Papa. 'She's been planning this trip for months, and now for her favouritest snack...she's willing to sacrifice it.'

I nodded as I stared at Papa and Dadi, the fiercest battle of wills.

The stare-off was decided by Mummy, who strode out of the car, took Dadi by the arm, and neatly popped her onto the back seat. Papa had no choice but to follow.

We waved as the car backed and then turned onto the main road. 'Bye, get some Gems,' I yelled.

'Ewww,' Rinki said. 'You get Skittles there, not Gems. Those are only in the desi shops. And anyway, you can buy Skittles here. Don't ask for anything, it's rude.'

I scowled at Rinki. She knew I meant those only. The car sped off, and we loped back into the house, Catrina threading between our legs, mewing desolately.

A few hours later, Mummy and Papa arrived, looking like our Wonder Mop, which wrung itself dry and came out from the bucket looking all twisted and bedraggled.

'How will she go with that puffed rice?' Papa was still muttering. 'That too in a plastic bag, it looks so bad.'

'She will manage.' Mummy was clearly fed up of this topic.

'How!' Papa sank into his favourite rocking chair. 'She doesn't speak a word of English, and the airline crew will only assist with baggage and all. They're not going to defend her right to carry puffed rice. I don't even think it's a right. I am sure it's not even a privilege. And did you see the quantity she carried?'

'Yes, it was like Santa's bag of toys,' I helpfully stepped in.

Rinki frowned at me. I frowned back at her. Santa is real, she can keep her opinions to herself.

Papa sighed, 'It really was, and in plastic!'

'At least it was double plastic,' Mummy said. She was doing a terrible job at suppressing a giggle.

Many hours later, Papa's phone rang. Dadi's face filled the screen. 'I am in Paris,' she said in Gujarati. 'Battery is low, I am putting phone down.'

'But what about the puffed rice?' Papa asked quickly. But Dadi had hung up on him. Papa tried calling back, but her phone was switched off.

He looked up, Mummy came out from the bedroom holding Dadi's mobile phone charger. 'She forgot to pack her charger.'

'I think she removed it,' Rinki said. 'She said she wanted to make space for the khakhras and thepla. She was complaining that the charger took up a lot of space.'

'That's why the diaper bag was so heavy! Khakhras and thepla!' Papa said. 'But how can her battery be so low?'

'Candy Crush,' I said helpfully. Again no one looked amused. But Dadi was an ace at that candy-smashing game, so much so that she would always be one of the top five players in the world. The leader board would read something like this:

1. Green Cheese
2. JackieC
3. Yashodhra

4. Farhan (not Akhtar, I checked)
5. ErikaRoks

And so the wait began, for Dadi to finally reach America. There was no way of reaching her until she called. Even though the flight offered Wi-Fi in pockets.

Mummy checked online and said, 'Her flight has landed.'

Every few minutes, Papa began checking his mobile phone. 'She's still not called.' He would turn to Rinki or me, thrust his phone in our hands, and ask, 'Do I have network?'

He did. Each time.

Finally, Mummy said, 'I will call Sandhya.'

Mummy dialled Sandhya Fui, who of course did not answer.

Papa looked at Mummy desperately. 'She must have got stopped at Immigration or Customs. I knew it. I told her not to take the puffed rice. It has such a strong smell also. That hing.'

'Don't be ridiculous, I am calling Jimmy.' She called our Fua who answered immediately.

‘Hang on,’ he said. ‘I’m putting you on speaker. We’re driving home.’

‘I have reached,’ Dadi’s voice filtered through. Papa and Mummy’s shoulders sagged in relief collectively. Rinki rolled her eyes and mouthed, I told you so. She totally had not!

‘Why didn’t you call? We’ve been so worried. How was the flight? Was everything okay? Did you face any trouble? Did the bags arrive safely?’ Questions poured out faster than pollution from a car exhaust pipe.

Sandhya Fui stepped in, ‘Oh all good, you all worry too much. What for? She came out smoothly, sailed through Immigration.’

‘Except—’ Jimmy Fua interjected.

‘Except what?’ Papa yelled.

‘Except she was carrying some plastic bag, and now that it’s been banned they wouldn’t let it through.’

Papa and Mummy gasped.

‘It was okay only,’ Dadi said. ‘I didn’t understand, they kept pointing at my bag. I thought they wanted to eat some, so I removed a bit in one of the plates I was carrying. But again they pointed. Then I realized they don't like to eat with their hand, so I added a spoon. But they still said no. You didn't let me carry my fork, so I couldn't offer them that.'

Papa was looking more and more like Dadi's onion-skin oil, purple and livid. Luckily Dadi could not see him, it was a voice call.

'And then he made me open my suitcase also! He took the mango pickle jar I took for Jimmy.'

Mummy was muttering something. But Dadi was still talking.

'And he asked me something. But I couldn't understand. I kept saying aachar. So then he opened it and thrust his entire hand in before I could say anything. And his whole hand came out with masala and oil. I think he was really angry.

'You think?' Rinki giggled. 'You think!' Papa echoed.

'But then one of the officials knew Gujarati. She sent off the other officer, I think to wash his hands, and told me that plastic is no longer allowed. I have plastic, how can it not be allowed? Anyway, I was so tired, so I didn't tell her that. Also, because I had three extra dabbas in my bag, I put the puffed rice into all of those. And threw the plastic bag. I felt a little bad throwing the two bags, such a waste, I tell you. We need to save the planet, and not throw away good plastic. Anyway, I told you, baccha, no one would stop me. I even managed to take the pickle jar, though how to eat now, someone put their hand in it!'

Papa looked like he would faint any second. I put a cushion under him quickly, just in case for a soft landing.

'She kept THREE empty dabbas?' Mummy was clearly wondering how they snuck past her raptor eyes.

'Anyway, I have more plastic bags in my luggage. No one stopped that. So that's that.'

Everyone burst out laughing on the other side. Papa muttered hasty goodbyes and hung up.

I went back to my room, and hoped Dadi would be back soon with Skittles. Because when the apocalypse comes, I want to be stuck with her. She'd be the only one prepared.

The Case of the Poster Prankster

ASHOK RAJAGOPALAN

Nila's grandparents, Major Loganathan and Dr Vatsala, sat at the kitchen table, sipping on their afternoon tea when Nila walked in, her face scrunched up in frustration.

'What's wrong, Nila? Did someone steal your homework again? Or worse, your snacks?' Loganathan, or Thatha, with his beak-like nose, tall and lean figure and love for crime novels, was pretending to be an avatar of the famous detective, Sherlock Holmes these days, and sought cases to solve.

Nila rolled her eyes, 'No, Thatha. It's worse than that.' She pulled out a poster from her backpack and slammed it on the table. The poster was a photocopy with bold black letters that read 'Wanted: Andrew—False Friend and Snooty Fellow' and underneath, a cartoon of Andrew grinning widely and stupidly, with the words 'No reward for finding such a fake!' written below.

'Someone put up these mean posters all over our classroom. Can you guys help me figure out who did it?'

Thatha and Paati exchanged a glance before leaning in to examine the poster. Paati adjusted her glasses and clicked her tongue in disapproval while Thatha traced the letters of the mischievous message with his finger, narrowing his eyes.

'Wow, this is not nice at all,' Paati shook her head.

'Nefarious!' agreed Thatha. 'It says mean things about Andrew and makes him look like a bad person.'

'Yeah, it's really mean,' Nila frowned. Thatha put on a checked cap, which made him look more like the famous detective. His excuse was that it was his 'thinking cap'.

He leaned back in his chair, stroking his chin, 'Alright, now let's think. Who would want to do something like this to Andrew? The school bully? The canteen aunty mad at him because he complained about the sambar? Or maybe it's the work of a criminal mastermind, with an evil plan to bring down Andrew's good name. But it's a mistake to form a theory without facts. Do you have any facts?'

Nila could only add, 'I saw them on the walls of our classroom.'

Thatha stood up, a determined glint in his eye. 'Don't worry, Nila. We'll figure it out. You can ask around and collect all the clues you can. And with Paati's medical knowledge and my love for detective stories, we'll crack this case open like a coconut.'

Paati gave a sly grin, 'We'll be the dynamic duo solving this case, Logs.'

'Call me Sir Log, Vats.'

'Then I'll be Doctor Vatsal.'

'Then the game is afoot!' Nila laughed, grateful to have such funny and smart grandparents. 'Thanks, Sir Log and Doctor Vatsal! I knew I could count on you.'

'Okay, so tell me, how high up were the posters stuck?' asked Thatha, looking serious.

'I had to stand on my tiptoes to reach it, Thatha... Sir Log.'

'People, especially kids, usually stick posters a bit higher than their eye level, even more so when they're in a hurry. This means that the person who did this is very tall. You're not a short girl yourself, but you had to stand on tiptoes, didn't you? So we have a tall culprit.'

'Amazing deduction, Sir Log!' Nila clapped her hands.

'Elementary, my dear Nila. Now let's dust it for fingerprints. I will go bring my kit,' Sir Log rose from his armchair.

Nila was excited and asked 'Paati, Paati! Where did Thatha get a fingerprint kit from?'

'You'll see,' her grandmother answered with a smile. 'Now go change and I'll get your milk.'

Nila quickly changed and came back to see Sir Log ready with his fingerprint kit, which consisted of a box of things like powder from scraped pencil leads, talcum powder, a fuzzy makeup brush, scissors and tape.

'These will do,' Sir Log said, looking proud and holding up his makeshift kit. 'No need for fancy kits bought online.'

'Why two powders, Sir Log?'

'You use the white for dark surfaces and the black for light ones, my dear Nila. Let's get cracking on this case!'

Nila watched as Sir Log dusted the poster with black powder. He then blew gently to remove the excess powder. Nila held her breath as he looked through his magnifying glass. But unfortunately, there were no fingerprints to be found, just some smudges.

'Looks like we have a professional criminal on our hands,' Sir Log said, sounding disappointed, 'They probably wore gloves or something.' Nila couldn't help but giggle at the thought of a professional criminal going to such lengths just to pull a prank on her friend. Then her face dropped.

'What do we do now, Sir Log? We don't have any other clue!'

'If only this were done by hand...' Vatsala frowned, 'Then we could compare the handwriting of the suspects and solve the case in no time. But no, the criminal had to go and use a computer like a coward!'

Sir Log nodded.

'Indeed, my dear Dr Vatsal. It seems technology has made our job much harder.'

'Hey Logs, I mean Sir Log, what about the "tall boy" clue?' asked Vatsala.

'Tall person, please, Doctor,' said Sir Log. 'One mustn't always assume that criminals are male. Now, Nila, the criminal is the tall child of your class. Who is she or he?'

'That's great,' laughed Vatsala. 'It's the tall child. Case solved!'

'That's right, Vatsal!'

'Er, Sir Log and Doctor Vatsal?' Nila coughed. 'There are three tall children in class.'

'We should be thankful there aren't six,' Vatsala frowned.

'Keep an eye on them,' said Sir Log. 'Get their fingerprints anyway. And collect as many copies of this poster as you can find.'

'As Cinderella said,' Vatsala laughed, '"one day, the prints will come."'

Nila left for school the next day feeling like a fingerprint-finding ninja. She also felt a bit doubtful. 'Get their fingerprints,' her grandfather had said easily, but how? She could not walk up to her classmates and ask them for their prints, could she? As she entered the class she glanced at the back row where the tall children sat. Arif, Roshni and Diksh. The 'suspects' in this crime. Just then, Andrew, the 'victim', ran over to her.

'I suspect Arif did it,' Andrew whispered. 'He and I don't get along. In fact, when the teacher announced that I was the class topper, he didn't even congratulate me. I bet he's the one who put those wanted posters of me all over the classroom!'

'Ah ha!' Nila smiled, her mind racing. 'Now we have a motive for the crime!'

'What are you talking about? What motive?' Andrew looked confused.

'My grandparents and I are on the case,' Nila explained, trying to sound as professional as possible. 'We're going to figure out who did this. Can you help us by getting more copies of the poster? And I'll write down the name of the suspects and their motives in my notebook.'

Andrew nodded and ran off to gather more posters. Nila quickly opened her rough note and wrote down the names of the three suspects. Each suspect was given a page. Under Arif's name, she wrote 'Motive: hates Andrew.' How exciting! She was one step closer to solving this case, wasn't she?

Getting Arif's print was a piece of cassata. Nila slyly slipped her shiny new geometry box in front of him during break while he was chomping on potato chips like a hungry hippo. Before he could even say anything she had his greasy fingerprints all over the metal box.

But getting Diksh's fingerprints was a bit of a challenge. Nila wished she had brought a few more interesting items to catch the fingerprints of the remaining suspects. Then she remembered her book covers made of laminated brown paper. Diksh, though academically challenged in other subjects, was the Tamil prodigy of the sixth grade. Nila approached him with a few made-up doubts about their Tamil homework, pretending to be in a state of confusion and voila! She had a couple of clear fingerprints. But getting Roshni's proved to be impossible. She was constantly moving about, like a butterfly flitting from flower to flower. And when Nila finally managed to run Roshni to earth, the girl looked at the book with her hands behind her back. Andrew returned with just one copy of the poster. This was the one he had kept to be upset over.

'But I don't think it's of any use,' he said. He was such a negative fellow. Nila ended her detective work for that day.

'If it were one of the two boys, I wouldn't need this girl's prints at all,' Nila consoled herself. She took Andrew's fingerprint too, since he had handled the poster many times and cried over it.

Sir Log was really excited about the new fingerprints, like a kid on his birthday morning. Nila helped him transfer the fingerprints from the box and book to a notebook. All she had to do was dust the fingerprints, put tape on them, and finally stick the tape onto her notebook. She wrote the names of the people whom the fingerprints belonged to, under the prints.

Vatsala said, 'I think you like using the fingerprint kit more than solving the case.' Sir Log didn't say if that was true or not, but he was definitely having a blast.

Vatsala snapped pictures of all the prints with her trusty phone and sent them to her laptop. The three of them huddled over the laptop like a team of scientists, zooming in on the new prints and comparing them to the ones on the poster. One of the prints on the new poster was Andrew's and that was ignored. They compared the remaining one to the prints of the tall boys.

Finally Sir Log announced, 'It's not Arif or Diksh.'

'It must be Roshni then!' Nila jumped up and down. 'Didn't Sherlock Holmes say that if we eliminate nonsense, what remains is the answer?'

Her grandfather frowned.

'"If you eliminate the impossible, whatever remains, however improbable, must be the truth." That's what he said. Please don't misquote

Holmes, Nila. And we need more proof and a reason for why she did it before we can say it's Roshni.'

Vatsala said, 'We need to find a motive.' Nila sighed.

'I wish Arif was the one who did it; he had a good reason.' But she was still excited to see where this case will lead. She used Paati's phone to make a video call to Andrew.

She asked him if he had any problems with Roshni. He said, 'I don't have any problem with her. We are buddies. We help each other with homework, exams...But there's one thing. Biology Ma'am gave me extra marks for my neat diagrams and that helped me become the class topper. All Roshni can draw are sloppy cartoons, not neat diagrams.'

Nila's eyes widened and she said, 'Roshni must be green with envy...ohhhh!'

Andrew asked, 'Why are you opening and closing your mouth like a goldfish?'

Nila explained, 'Cartoons, extra marks. See? Skills and motive. She must have made those posters.'

'Oh she's not like that. Let me call and ask her.'

Nila quickly said, 'Wait, Andrew! We don't want to scare off our suspect before we have all the evidence.'

'Suspect? Ha, ha, fat chance!'

* * *

She reported the latest to her detective team.

'Looks like it's Roshni, after all,' declared Vatsala.

'Right, Dr Vatsal,' said Sir Log. 'We have motive, skills and a few clues. But, you know, she might have an alibi. We have to find out where she was when the crime took place.'

'Exactly, Sir Log! The time of crime,' Vatsala nodded. 'Nila, when did you all notice the posters? Was it after lunch?'

'No, Paati...Dr Vatsal. They were there when I went into class that morning. I was not the first; there were a few children there already. About five, looking at the posters and laughing. Roshni was there, laughing louder than the others. But I heard that she was not the first one to come in, either.'

'So!' said Sir Log. 'The crime was committed in the still and silent hours before students came in. Roshni could have come in, stuck the posters up, and left to the canteen or somewhere. Then she would have made an entry later, pretending that she was just coming to class. But how do we prove that?'

'What about the CCTV cameras in the corridor, Sir Log?' asked Nila. 'They will show who came in and when.'

'Wonderful, Nila!' Sir Log patted his granddaughter on the back. 'But you should have told me this earlier, my dear. My mind is stuck in the Sherlock Holmes period, and can never consider modern gadgets.'

'Then all Nila has to do is to look at the video footage and bring the criminal to justice!' Vatsal raised her hand to give her granddaughter a high-five.

'Hey! No!' Nila did not take the high-five. 'I can't do that! I can't go to the office room and ask to see the tapes. We have to think of something else.'

Next day, Nila and Andrew waited for Roshni in the canteen during lunch. As soon as she walked by, they pounced.

'Rosh, we know what you did,' said Andrew, holding up the poster.

Roshni looked at them with a smirk and said, 'Oh, you do? Tell me, detectives, what did I do? Steal the school's notice board? Put a cockroach in the sambar there?'

'Don't play dumb, Roshni,' Nila held up her notebook with Roshni's motive written in it.

'As if I have the time to make posters. I'm too busy saving the world one science problem at a time. And even if I did, who's going to believe you over me?'

Nila stepped forward and said, 'We'll see about that. You better come clean now, or we'll go straight to the principal. The CCTV footage will show you entered the classroom with a bunch of posters. You made these posters out of jealousy because Andrew got extra marks for his neat diagrams.'

Roshni let out a sigh and said, 'Oh, please. You have a wild imagination. No, I made the posters because I miss being friends with Andrew and I thought this would bring us closer together. Like a funny prank between friends.'

Nila and Andrew exchanged a glance and nodded. He smiled.

'Sorry, Rosh. I didn't know you felt that way. You see, after becoming the class topper for the first time in my life...'

'I thought you went all snooty, Andy. Will you help me draw better diagrams, please?'

Nila rolled her eyes, 'Ugh! You two go do that and I'll just go solve some other mystery. Like why the canteen idli is good but the sambar is not.'

Later, Sir Log, Dr Vatsala and Nila celebrated their victory with glasses of mango juice. 'Here's to the best detective team in the world,' Nila said.

A Photograph

RUSKIN BOND

Grandmother sat in a rocking-chair, under the mango tree. It was late summer and there were sunflowers in the garden and a warm wind in the trees. Grandmother was knitting me a pullover for the winter months. Her hair was white, her eyes were not very strong, but her fingers moved quickly with the needles, and the needles kept clicking till afternoon. Grandmother was old, but there were very few wrinkles on her skin.

In some of my tales I have perhaps been guilty of writing more admiringly of Grandfather than of Grandmother. It's true that Grandfather and I had much in common, and that he gave me more of his time, but then, he had more time to give. He was a retired gentleman. But housewives never retire. And Grandmother always had housework. She saw to our meals, she did the shopping, kept the household accounts, and dealt with a variety of tradesmen, including the butcher, the baker, the dhobi, and various egg, fruit, vegetable and charcoal vendors.

And so, if our pets sometimes hindered her in the efficient running of the house, who can blame her for being a little short with us at times?

In the long run, though Grandmother grumbled, she always tolerated most of our pets. She nursed Toto the monkey when he was sick. She was fond of the Hornbill; in fact, she liked all birds. She kept her own birdbath in the garden, where mynas, thrushes, bulbuls and flower-peckers would come for a dip or a drink, and she never forgot to fill the stone bath with fresh water in the mornings.

When she did find time to relax in her rocking-chair, she liked having me beside her, and she liked talking about her youth.

One afternoon, after lunch (or tiffin, as we called it then), I was rummaging in a box of old books and family heirlooms that I had found in the box room. There was not much to interest me except a book on butterflies, and as I was going through it I found a small photograph in between the pages. It was a faded picture, a little yellow and foggy—a picture of a girl standing against a wall; and from the other side of the wall a pair of hands reached up, as though someone were about to climb it. There were flowers growing near the girl, but I could not tell what they were; there was a small tree, too, but it was just a tree to me.

I ran out into the garden.

'Granny!' I shouted. 'Look at this picture! I found it in that box of old things. Whose picture is it?'

I raised myself on the arm of the rocking-chair, and nearly toppled over into a bed of nasturtiums.

'Now look what you have gone and done,' said Grandmother. 'I've lost count of my stitches. The next time you jump up like that, I'll make you finish the pullover yourself.'

Grandmother was always threatening to teach me how to knit. She said it would take my mind off unhealthy creatures like frogs and lizards and buffaloes. Once, when Toto tore the drawing room curtains, she put a needle and thread in my hand and made me stitch the curtain together, even though I made long, two-inch stitches which had to be taken out by Grandmother and done all over again.

She took the photograph from my hand, and we both stared at it for quite some time. The girl had long, loose hair, and she wore a long dress that nearly covered her ankles, and sleeves that reached her wrists; but, in spite of the all drapery, the girl appeared to be full of freedom and movement; she stood with her legs apart and her hands on her hips, and she had a wide, almost devilish smile on her face.

'Whose picture is it?' I asked.

'A little girl's, of course,' said Grandmother. 'Can't you tell?'

'Yes, but did you know her?'

'Oh yes, I knew her,' said Grandmother. 'But she was a wicked little girl, and I shouldn't tell you about her. I'll tell you about the photograph. It was taken in our home, oh many many years ago, and that's the garden wall, and over the wall there was a road leading to town. That girl used to sneak over the wall sometimes, and visit the bazar. She couldn't resist jalebis. Do you like jalebis?'

'Yes, very much! But whose hands are they?' I asked. 'Coming up from the other side?'

Grandmother squinted and looked closely at the picture, shaking her head. 'It's the first time I noticed,' she said. 'They must have been a child's. Another child's.'

'Were they Grandfather's? Didn't he climb over the wall, afterwards?'

'No, nobody climbed up. At least, I don't remember.'

'And you remember well, Granny.'

'Yes, I remember...I remember what is not in the photograph. It was a spring day, and there was a cool breeze blowing. Those flowers at the girl's feet, they were marigolds, and the bougainvillaea creeper was a mass of purple. You can't see those colours in the photo, and even if you could, you wouldn't be able to smell the flowers or feel the breeze.'

'And what about the girl?' I asked. 'Tell me about the girl.'

'Well, she was a wicked girl,' said Grandmother. 'You don't know the trouble her mother had getting her into those fine clothes she's wearing.'

'They're terrible clothes,' I said.

'She thought so, too. Most of the time she hardly wore a thing. Dehra Dun summers were as hot then as they are now. She used to go swimming in the canal. The neighbours were shocked. Boys never teased her, because she didn't hesitate to fight them!'

'She looks tough,' I said. 'You can tell by the way she's smiling. At any moment something's going to happen.'

'Something *did* happen,' said Grandmother. 'Her mother wouldn't let her get out of those awful clothes, so she jumped into the canal fully clothed!'

I burst into laughter, and Grandmother joined in.

‘Who was the girl?’ I asked. ‘You must tell me who she was.’

‘No, that wouldn’t do,’ said Grandmother. ‘I won’t tell you.’

I knew the girl in the photograph was really Grandmother, but I pretended not to know. I knew, because Grandmother still smiled in the same way.

‘Come on, Granny,’ I said. ‘Tell me, tell me.’

But Grandmother shook her head and carried on with her knitting, and I held the photograph in my hands, looking from it to my grandmother and back again, trying to find points in common between the old lady and the little pigtailed girl. A lemon-coloured butterfly settled on the end of Grandmother’s knitting needle, and stayed there while the needle clicked away. I made a grab at the butterfly, and it flew off in a dipping flight and settled on a sunflower.

‘I wonder whose hands they were,’ whispered Grandmother to herself, with her head bowed in memory, and her needles clicking away in the soft, warm silence of that summer afternoon.

Travelling with Detective Dida

BULBUL SHARMA

The train slowed down and then gathered speed again. I rubbed the dusty window pane and peered out. We were passing through a dense jungle with trees that seemed to hug each other. Far away, I could see a silver line glittering in the dim green light. I realized, as we left it behind, that it must have been a waterfall flowing down giant rocks. I wished I could have jumped out and had a quick shower in that clear, sparkling water. It was so hot and muggy in our compartment. 'We must be near Raipur. Only four hours left for Durg,' muttered Dida, my grandmother. She was sitting up straight on the seat, her tiny round glasses perched on the edge of her nose. 'What is a treacle tart?' she asked me.

My grandmother was teaching herself English from an old school book of mine. My grandmother, my sister Radha and I were travelling from Calcutta to Durg, a long train journey of thirty hours through the plains of central India. We crossed flowing rivers, dense jungles and bleak ravines where jackals howled at the passing train. Once I thought I saw a tiger standing near a pool of water but my grandmother, whose eyes were very sharp, said it was a hyena. 'Too small to be a tiger,' she said, looking up briefly from her book. 'It could be a very young tiger,' I argued.

'Could be an underfed tiger,' mumbled my sister from the top berth. She had curled up there as soon as we got into the train and only came down once to go to the bathroom and once to pick up a big box of chips. I could hear her munching away and it made me feel very irritated since I had already finished my share of chips.

This was many, many years ago and the chips we ate were homemade and packed in little cardboard boxes.

I am a grandmother myself now with grown-up grandkids, but I still remember that train journey: the smell of coal dust, the taste of the food Dida kept bringing out from the huge tiffin carrier and the chaos that erupted when she caught the book thief. That journey with my Dida remains so fresh in my mind and I often go back to visit it and get lost in the misty times of the past.

We had almost missed our train since there was a huge traffic jam on the Howrah Bridge in Calcutta. 'Shall we get down and walk to the station?' asked Dida. 'How can we do that? You have so much luggage, Ma. It seems to me that you are going for a year instead of just one month,' my uncle said, keeping an eye on the slow-moving traffic. 'You know that you get nothing in that wretched place your brother has chosen to live in,' she grumbled. When we finally got into the train compartment, my grandmother ordered the porter to settle our five suitcases and her various parcels under the berth. After a brief argument with him, my grandmother told my uncle to pay him. Then she turned to the tall, gawky boy, our cook's son, who was also travelling with us. 'Make sure you do not get down at any smaller stations till we reach Durg,' she told him sternly. The boy, whose name was Mohan, grinned and scampered off to the next compartment.

'I am sure we will never see him again,' said my sister cheerfully.

The train began moving and my uncle quickly touched my grandmother's feet. 'Go. Go,' she shouted at him and gave him a push. He jumped off the moving train and then we saw him laughing as he stumbled. 'Always was clumsy, even as a child,' muttered Dida as she began sorting out her luggage. The giant tiffin carrier was placed in one corner and a cloth draped over it to protect it from the coal dust. It began to sway as the train gathered speed, looking like a small, shrouded gnome about to stroll away any minute.

Radha and I took out our books and Dida took out my old, tattered rapid English reader. We all settled down in our corners. Luckily no one else had booked the fourth berth in our compartment. It was a lovely feeling at first to know we had thirty hours ahead of us. We could read so many books undisturbed; little did we know what was going to happen next.

Soon we left the green paddy fields, coconut trees and sparkling ponds behind and then the landscape gradually became dry and brown. The rocking movement of the train was making me feel sleepy. We had been eating continuously ever since we had left Howrah Station. As soon as our train left Calcutta, Dida took the cover off the tiffin carrier. Then she detached two steel plates from it like a magician. She heaped potato and cauliflower wrapped in soft luchis on the plates along with some fried vegetables and spoonfuls of tomato chutney. The train was travelling really fast and the food slid all over the plate but we managed to finish everything. Dida made us wipe the plates and then she put some sweets on them. 'Eat, eat quickly. The next station will come soon and some greedy, strange person might come in here,' she said, looking around suspiciously. Her own special food was packed in a cloth bag and she dipped into it sparingly.

I was happily dozing, dreaming of oceans and rivers, when suddenly a shout woke me up. 'Thief! There is a thief on this train. Someone has stolen my newspaper. Call the T.C. Where is the T.C.?' a man was shouting as he ran down the corridor, banging on the doors. Dida got up at once. She adjusted her saree and pushing her glasses firmly on her nose, she went out. 'What happened?' she asked the T.C. The ticket collector was a young man with a long nose that was twitching nervously. 'Not sure, Ma. This gentleman is saying someone stole his newspaper and the lady is saying someone took her books.'

Dida narrowed her eyes and looked at the ticket collector who was wringing his hands and decided she would take matters in her own capable hands. She marched out into the corridor.

My sister and I quickly followed. This was going to be exciting—we knew from past experience with my grandmother. There was no problem she could not solve; no mystery she could not unravel effortlessly.

'Now tell me one by one what items have been stolen. Mira, write it down,' she said in a firm voice.

By now the people in all the various compartments had come out. They stared at Dida with awe. I forgot to tell you that my grandmother was very tall and wore her long white hair in a thick plait that reached down to her waist. She always dressed in a white cotton saree that was starched so stiffly that from far she looked like the mast of a small boat. The passengers gave a list of the missing items.

I wrote them down as quickly as I could.

1. One Agatha Christie novel titled *Sleeping Murder*
2. Two Bengali magazines
3. Three newspapers
4. 5 children's books

Titles
The Sea of Adventure
Uncle Tom's Cabin

David Copperfield
The Clever Mouse and the Foolish Hare
Folk Tales of Bengal

'All this went missing in the last three hours?' asked Dida and the passengers nodded, glaring at the ticket collector who looked down at his feet, his nose twitching even more furiously.

'Did anyone get on or get off at any of the stations we have passed till now?' Dida asked him, her voice surprisingly gentle.

'No, Ma. Look, I have a list of stations and names of passengers,' he said, showing her a long sheet of paper.

Dida took a quick look. I wanted to see it too but she folded it and gave it back to the T.C.

'Now, if you don't mind. We should do a quick search of every compartment. Since no one has got on or off the train, I think the thief is still amongst us,' said Dida.

At first there was a faint protest by some of the passengers but when Dida fixed her famous 'I will stand no nonsense' look on them, they reluctantly agreed. There were six compartments, if I remember correctly. The first compartment we went into was occupied by a very old and very deaf couple and their equally aged servant. They were not sure what was going on and kept asking if we had reached Jabalpur. We apologized and left them in peace. The next compartment looked more promising since it was filled with four men playing cards. They looked up guiltily as soon as Dida knocked and entered. 'Harmless fun. It helps to pass the long journey,' one of them said, quickly putting the playing cards away. The search revealed a few bottles with red liquid but no books or magazines.

'I don't think they have ever read a book in their lives,' muttered Dida as she shut the door.

Then in the third compartment we struck lucky. One newspaper, crumpled and wet, was found under the berth.

'I have no idea how it got here,' said the poor, distraught lady staring at the evidence. Her husband, who had been rudely woken up, glared at us.

'Take it away. Dirty rag,' he growled.

'How did it get here?' I asked Dida but she seemed to be lost in thought and did not reply.

In the fourth compartment, the parents with five kids who had lost all the children's books were sitting looking gloomy.

The children were fighting amongst themselves and their mother looked exhausted.

'There is no point in searching this one,' said Dida and marched into the next one. A barking sound greeted us as the door opened slightly. 'Sorry, you cannot come in. We are resting,' said a man's voice.

'How can you rest with that dog barking away?' asked Dida. She knocked loudly again. The dog now went mad and began scratching at the door. In fact, it was the dog who managed to slide open the door of thc compartment. We looked in.

And there was our culprit.

Newspapers lay torn in shreds and the books, luckily unharmed, were piled up on the berth. The dog was sitting on a torn magazine, chewing one corner delicately. He stopped and began barking at us but it was a happy, welcoming bark.

'What have you to say about this?' asked Dida, pointing an accusing finger at the dog's master.

'Bimbo cannot help it. He was born a book thief. Always stealing books wherever we go. Other dogs steal slippers but Bimbo only likes to chew paper. We try to control him but he goes mad locked up during a train journey. Anyway, you people should be more careful about your books and newspapers. Why leave them lying about for my dog to pick them up?' asked the man aggressively.

'You must control your dog. You will buy five children's books at the next station and also two newspapers and magazines, if you can find them,' ordered Dida. The man was about to protest but then our timid T.C. suddenly sprang to life.

'Sir, your dog should have been on a leash. You must do what this lady says or pay a fine to the Railways.'

'Alright,' said the man. We all looked at Bimbo who had stopped chewing the magazine and was happily wagging his tail. He gave us a lopsided grin as if to say 'Why blame me?'

I felt sorry for the book thief.

'How old is the dog?' asked Dida

'Eight months,' said the man, grumpily.

'Give him some carrots to chew and a hard rag ball. He will stop stealing paper then. He just wants to chew something,' said Dida as she walked out.

By the time we reached the next big station, three hours later since the train was running late, Dida had made a beautiful rag ball out of an old gamcha she was carrying with her. She tore strips and tied them up tightly with the string she found wrapped around her various parcels. The man was very pleased and Bimbo was thrilled with the rag ball. He sat down at once with his new toy, ignoring the torn magazine under his paws. The children were pleased too since they had been given new books at Jabalpur station.

'We had finished reading the old ones. Thanks to Bimbo we got new ones,' they said to me. Mohan had brought us all laddoos and hot jalebis to celebrate.

Dida settled down once more with her rapid English reader. The train hurried through the vast arid landscape of central India and we went back to reading our books. I forgot to tell you that we too had got new books thanks to Bimbo.

'What is a treacle tart?' Dida asked me again.

I only found out the answer to that question twenty years later but by then, my Dida, whom I loved so much, had gone to live with the stars. I am sure she gets lots of delicious treacle tarts to eat there as she goes around solving mysteries in the skies.

Dadu and Jack

SWAPNA DUTTA

It was one of those Sunday afternoons when the sound of falling rain seemed to have driven out all other sounds and it felt like one big washing day. My sister and I, tired of playing Ludo and Snakes & Ladders, were just thinking about what to do next. In those days our modes of entertainment were limited, there being no mobiles, Internet or quite so many indoor games as now. Little girls played with dolls while those fond of reading turned to their favourite books invariably. So my sister brought down her dolls and I was lost in one of the Famous Five adventures. Grandma, or Mamoi, as we called her, was turning out cupboards upstairs and Grandpa, or Dadu, was hunting for something in the attics. He finally came down lugging a

Victorian easy-chair that had been reposing amidst a pile of unused furniture. I remember that afternoon so clearly because that was the time he told us about Jack and how he became part of our family.

I had grown up hearing stories about Jack, the tiger cub, whom Dadu had brought home unexpectedly one evening and refused to part with. Jack's various exploits became a part of our family history. But it was always the others who spoke to me of Jack—my mother, my aunt and my grandma. Dadu never spoke of him. And somehow I could never ask him directly about his unusual pet. I felt instinctively that the memory would hurt him. But that afternoon as he sat on the long unused chair he suddenly looked up and said, 'Did you know that I lay on this easy-chair the whole night, the night I brought Jack home?' my sister and I jumped up, clamouring for the story. And he told us.

It happened a long, long time ago when Dadu was a young officer, working among the tribals of Chotanagpur, as it was called then. The place was very different from what it is now, being chockfull of deep forests and trees growing wild. There was no electricity, no taps or running water and no railway tracks for miles around. There were no proper roads in the forests either. In most of the places the trees grew so close together that not even a jeep could pass through. In any case, very few people dared to venture into the dense forest teeming with wild animals—tigers, cheetahs, leopards, wolves, bison, deer and what have you! Incidentally, those were the days when cheetahs (now said to be extinct) still roamed around and were fairly common. The only way to reach some of these places where the tribals lived was on horseback. And that too only if one really knew the way! It is easy to get lost in the forest and go round and round in circles.

Dadu always rode when he entered these forests. He always said that there was no question of his getting lost because he knew the Chotanagpur forests like the back of his hand. And being a crack shot, he was not afraid of wild animals either. Needless to say, anyone going there had to be well armed. That day, when Dadu reached the little tribal settlement in the heart of the forest, a terror-stricken group confronted him. Three little children had been bodily lifted and dragged away by an enormous Royal Bengal tiger during that week and were never heard of again. Moreover, they were afraid that the tiger was a badly wounded one, shot at by a European big game hunter. Hunting was not forbidden by law in those days. Dadu frowned when he heard this. A wounded tiger is ten times more dangerous than an ordinary one. Crazy with the pain of the wound, it was doubly ferocious. He realized that it was positively dangerous to leave it hanging around. Too many lives were at stake! The people begged him to track the wounded tiger and kill it before it could attack anyone else.

Dadu set off at once. It was not difficult to trace the wounded tiger because there was a thick trail of blood all the way. But when he finally located it by the riverside, it was already dead. It was actually a tigress and not a tiger and beside her enormous bulk lay three little newborn cubs, their eyes tightly shut. Dadu jumped down from his horse and was beside them in a jiffy. Two of the cubs were dead too. But the third one shivered and tried to move. It was a bitterly cold, grey December afternoon. Dadu picked up the cub and cuddled it in his arms. Gradually the little cub stopped shivering and fell asleep.

The tribals were astonished when they saw the bundle in his arms.

'Surely you don't mean to take it back with you?' the tribal leader, known as the mukhiya, asked him in an incredulous voice. 'It may be quite harmless at the moment but it is a tiger after all! And tigers are natural enemies of human beings.'

'I don't know about that,' said Dadu quite firmly, 'But I am taking it back. I shall certainly not leave it stranded here on its own to die like the other two.'

'But it is not your responsibility!' remarked another elderly tribal. 'It's not as if you killed its mother! In any case it is better for it to die or else it may kill you when it gets a little older.'

Dadu did not bother to reply. He took off the sweater he was wearing and bundled the cub in it. Then he jumped up on his horse, holding the cub with one hand and the reins with the other.

'You are crazy!' shouted the mukhiya. 'You can't possibly ride like that the whole way. It will take you ages if you do. Moreover, how on earth are you going to defend yourself against wild animals you are sure to come across? You can't hold the reins and the cub and aim your gun at the same time!'

For a moment Dadu was taken aback. What the mukhiya said was true enough. He couldn't really hope to reach home without coming across a couple of leopards at least, if not other animals twice as dangerous. But he did not change his mind. 'I'll cross the bridge when I come to it,' he told himself.

Perhaps Dadu had never prayed for a safe journey before. He loved and enjoyed facing adventures. But as he rode that evening in the fast approaching twilight holding the little motherless mite in one arm, he prayed like never before that he might make it to the town in safety. And he did! For once he had no need to use his gun on his way. But naturally it took him much longer to reach home. By the time he stabled his horse and strode into the house the stars were already out and Mamoi had just finished lighting the lamps. She looked curiously at the bundle in his arms.

'What have you got there?' she asked.

Dadu laid the bundle on the sofa.

'Good gracious! It's a cat!' cried Mamoi. 'How could you? You know we don't need any more animals in the house. We have more than enough!'

Dadu paid no heed to her words. 'Is there any warm milk? If not, you'd better heat some and bring it in a saucer.'

'I can't think what possessed you to fetch a cat from the woods—of all things! And that too, a horrid tabby cat!' Mamoi grumbled. But when she fetched the milk, the cub was unable to lap it.

'Do you have any of the feeding bottles belonging to the girls?' asked Dadu.

'After all these years?' cried Mamoi, amazed. 'Talk sense! What do you want it for, anyway?

Kittens can always fend for themselves. It will soon lap up all of it,'

'I'll have to buy a bottle then,' said Dadu. 'And incidentally, Jack is not a cat. He is a tiger cub. A Royal Bengal tiger.'

'W-H-A-T!' screamed Mamoi, dropping the lamp in her nervousness. A cat was bad enough but a TIGER! It couldn't bear thinking of! But Dadu was already out of the house to buy a feeding bottle.

I don't quite know how long it took my grandfather to reconcile his wife to the idea of having Jack in the house. Probably when my mother came home from her residential school for the weekend, she had firmly put her oar in. And so did my aunt who was newly married. Anyway, Jack stayed put, loved and petted by all. He played and roamed all about the house with the two dogs, washed his face when they did and curled up on the carpet beside them. At first he lived on milk and rice. But once on a meat diet, he grew by leaps and bounds.

In a short time, there was no mistaking Jack for anything but what he actually was—a tiger cub. He also developed a really fierce growl. Most outsiders were terrified of him and avoided our house like plague! All of a sudden the garden and orchards were totally free of sneak thieves. Instead there seemed to be a crowd outside the gate at all hours with people peering over to catch a glimpse of Jack. People who had seldom visited us before also turned up at our gate saying, 'Mr Sen, we hear you've got a pet tiger in the house? Is it really true? Can we see him from a distance?'

Dadu had not bargained for all this publicity and found it quite exasperating, especially because everyone seemed to have a piece of advice for him as to how he should bring up a tiger. And he had to lock Jack up in a room when they came because Jack did not like strangers.

Needless to say, Jack loved Dadu more than anyone else and followed him about all over the place, including the garden. When Dadu sat at his table working, Jack lay curled up at his feet. When he reclined in his easy chair reading the newspaper, Jack sat huddled up next to him. He growled at times but the family and servants were used to his sudden fits of temper. But one day Dadu had to go off to the forest for the entire day for some important work and could not scoot home during lunch break as he usually did. Which meant he was unable to feed Jack himself. One of the servants carried his meal, probably a tad too late. Jack was so angry that he jumped on him terrifying him to bits and thumped his paw so hard on the bowl that it became flat like a saucer.

Dadu was worried when he came home and heard about it. After all, it would hardly be possible for him to be home during Jack's feeding time every day and he did not want any accidents to happen. But one did happen soon after. A straying goat sneaked into the garden and Jack pounced on it and would have killed it if Dadu hadn't reached the place just then. To cap it all, Dadu's transfer orders to a big and busy town came the very same evening. The quarters allotted to him was large enough but had no compound and was on a noisy street. He was off his head with worry. 'We can't take Jack with us,' he told Mamoi. 'It would be cruel to keep him locked up all the time. He would be downright miserable.'

'But what are we to do?' asked Mamoi. 'I can't think of a single person who would agree to keep him or love him like we do. As it is, people think we are quite crazy to keep a tiger in the house.'

'Should I take him back to the forest and leave him there?' asked Dadu and added, 'No, I can't do that!'

'Why not?' asked Mamoi. 'It seems the most sensible thing to do and our only option.'

'No,' said Dadu firmly, 'It's out of the question.'

Hunting was not only not forbidden at the time but was also in great vogue. The forests were often visited by game hunters, mostly foreigners. Dadu couldn't face the thought of some game hunter killing Jack just for sport.

'We have to give him to a zoo in that case,' said Mamoi. 'At least he will be fed and looked after and have as much space as he is used to.'

'I suppose it is the only thing to do,' said Dadu sadly.

There was hardly any time to lose. Dadu set the ball rolling and made arrangements with the Alipore zoo in Calcutta to have him sent there. He tried to postpone his transfer as long as he could but the day Jack left had to be faced. He could never forget the look of hurt bewilderment in Jack's eyes when he was obliged to leave for his new home. Dadu's colleagues, who always said that he had nerves of steel and nothing ever upset him, were stunned to see his streaming eyes after Jack left. For quite some time no one dared to mention Jack's name in Dadu's hearing. After his transfer, Dadu was too busy with his new job and could not manage a trip to Calcutta. But he got news of Jack through letters, having requested a few relatives and friends to enquire about Jack in the Alipore zoo.

When he could finally manage to make a trip to Calcutta he made off for the zoo at once. He dashed off to the tiger's cage. But there was no Jack there!

'Jack!' he cried, looking about him frantically, 'Jack! Jack!' An enormous tiger—twice the size he had been a few months ago—dashed out of his den and stood before Dadu, trying to get at him through the bars. When he couldn't, he lay down on the floor in front of him just as he used to do at home. By then there was a huge crowd near Dadu, staring at the amazing scene. But Dadu couldn't care less! Jack was here and seemed to be well. That was all that mattered.

The keeper of the tigers landed up to see what the hullaballoo was about. He stared incredulously at Dadu and Jack. 'Do you know this tiger?' he asked surprised.

'I do. He was mine,' said Dadu, 'Will you let me in for a moment and allow me to stroke him just once? I don't want to break rules.' The keeper looked at him keenly and let him in. Jack rushed to Dadu and rubbed his head against his feet as he purred (or should I say roared?) loudly. Dadu stroked him and cuddled him but only for a moment. He did not want to get the keeper into trouble.

Dadu went home happy and planned to bring Mamoi and his daughters along to see Jack the next morning. But there was an urgent telegram from office waiting for him and he had to rush back to his place of work the same night. It was more than a month before he could manage to visit Calcutta again. But when he went to the zoo there was no Jack to greet him. The keeper informed him that he had been sent to the London zoo a week before. And Dadu never saw Jack again.

Dadu's voice was strained as he ended his tale and stood up. His eyes were full of tears. I felt a strange lump in my throat and my sister blinked. The rain had stopped outside but everything seemed glum and desolate. I wondered if it was nature's way of sharing our mood.

A note about the story and my grandfather

This is a true story, written down from memory as I heard it from my grandfather, grandmother and my mother. I still have some photos of Jack taken by my grandfather and one of Jack with my grandmother. They are among my most precious possessions.

The events described in this story are from nearly a century ago, when laws about wild animals were very different from what they are today. Now, there would probably be an animal shelter managed by the forest department that would take in an orphaned animal. Studies have shown now that wild animals need to stay in the wild as much as possible. But those were different times, and men like my grandfather would do anything to save the animals in need that came their way.

My grandfather Bijoy Kanta Sen was a remarkable man in many ways. Having graduated from the Presidency College, Calcutta, he joined Bihar Civil Service like his uncle (father's younger brother) who had brought him up. It was at his place that he learned horse riding and also shooting. He soon became an avid horse rider and also a crack shot. His senior officers soon realized this and sent him out to faraway places where there were no proper roads and one could only reach there on horseback. He was totally fearless.

There was another side to his character. Being a student of literature, Dadu was an avid reader and always made time for reading when he was at home. Ever since I can remember, his house was chockfull of books, which included the complete works of Leo Tolstoy and Victor Hugo (who were his special favourites), complete works of Dickens, Conan Doyle and other famous writers of his time. Also bound volumes of *The Strand Magazine*. As my grandmother also loved reading, there were all the Bengali classics as well. Both of them encouraged us (my sister and I) to read right from our childhood.

Grandfather led a very disciplined life, getting up at the crack of dawn and drawing water from the well himself, he had his bath before anyone else was awake. Having lived with his father in the village during his schooldays, he was familiar with Sanskrit and read parts of the Gita and the Chandi first thing in the morning and went off to tend his garden before the rest of us were awake. He led a very active life until he fell really ill with cancer and passed away at the age of eighty-two.

A 'Typical' Vacation

NANDINI NAYAR

Sarika had a theory. She kept it buried because she was afraid of what would happen if she said it out loud. But when she heard that she and Sachin were spending the winter break with Aba-Aaji, she forgot this and said, 'But they hate us!'

'Sarika,' Aai laughed. 'Aba-Aaji don't hate you.'

'Then why haven't we gone to Nagpur for ages?' Sarika demanded.

The last time Sarika had visited her grandparents had been after her seventh birthday.

'Between my job, travel, summer camps... where was the time?' Aai asked. 'Now they want you to stay with them when Baba and I travel.'

Other people's grandparents visited regularly. Why didn't theirs?

'It's because of their garden!' Aai said. 'They can't leave it so they hardly go anywhere.'

Then Sarika brought out her trump card. 'They weren't nice to us when we met at that wedding last year,' she said. 'Aba told Sachin to stop playing games. And Aaji shouted at me... said I was always on my phone!'

'But you do spend a lot of time on your phone!'

'I was texting Trisha!' Sarika protested.

'Aba-Aaji don't understand computer games or texting,' Aai explained. 'We didn't have it when your Maushi and I were growing up.'

'We could stay with Priya Maushi when you are away,' Sarika suggested. But Maushi was travelling and her son Piyush would be in Nagpur too.

'Aaji doesn't like Piyush either,' Sarika said. Aai laughed. 'It's true!' Sarika insisted. 'She snatched his book away and wouldn't return it!'

'She thinks he spends too much time reading,' Aai said.

If only there was someone else they could stay with! But Dada-Dadi lived with Satish Kaka in the US, so Aba-Aaji's house was the only option.

Trisha made sympathetic noises when Sarika reported this. 'Tell me everything!' she said. 'Every. Thing!'

But how? Aai had made Sarika leave her phone behind because she said the coverage at Aba-Aaji's house wasn't good. And because she thought Sarika would be too busy to text.

Sarika wished Aai could see how free she was in Nagpur and how bored. Aba-Aaji had tried to get them to climb trees, water the garden and now Aaji peeped in to ask, 'Want to help Aba dig up vegetables?'

'I don't like digging,' Sachin explained. 'I like games. On the TV or laptop.'

But Sachin's games had been left behind because Aai said the power often went off at Aba-Aaji's.

'Have you tried digging?' Aaji asked.

They hadn't. 'But I know I won't like it,' Sachin added.

'Then you can lay the table for lunch,' Aaji said briskly.

They found Piyush wiping plates. 'Here,' he offered Sachin a towel. Sachin ignored it because T-shirts worked just as well as towels. Piyush stared at him rubbing a plate with his T-shirt and broke into giggles. Sarika was surprised because Piyush always looked so scared. Perhaps he simply needed someone to talk to.

'Where are your books?' Sarika asked. 'Mumma forgot to pack them,' he said. He sounded so mournful that Sachin stopped wiping a spoon to ask, 'Do you miss books *that* much?'

Piyush nodded. Sarika caught the glint of tears and said, 'Aai says they had lots of books when they were little. Some of them must be around.'

'I'll help you look,' Sachin offered. But Piyush couldn't wait. While they were clearing lunch, he sneaked away.

'Put the rice in this bowl,' Aba told Sachin.

'Why?' Sachin demanded.

'Because we put food away in smaller vessels,' Aba explained.

Sachin was baffled. 'Aai doesn't,' he muttered.

'She does,' Aaji told him. 'Every day!'

Sarika, pouring the dal into a bowl, paused. Did Aai do that? Sachin looked at her and she shrugged. At home, they escaped as soon as a meal was done, Sachin to play and Sarika to moan to Trisha about the food she'd just eaten. Discussions about leftovers were beyond them.

'Why don't you sit under the trees?' Aba suggested when the kitchen was clean.

'Why?'

'Why what?'

'Why should we sit under a tree?' Sachin asked.

'Because it's nice,' Aba said.

'It's nice *here*,' Sachin pointed out. Aba waited to see if they really meant it and then went away.

'But what will we do?' Sarika moaned.

'Look at the TV,' Sachin said bitterly, 'and think about all the things we could have been watching or playing!' The TV in Aba-Aaji's house didn't work.

'Why don't you get it fixed?' Sachin demanded. No one would come all this way to repair it, Aba-Aaji said. Besides, they didn't watch TV.

'What, not even the news?' Sarika asked. Didn't grown-ups *like* the news?

Aba-Aaji though it was too noisy. 'We like to listen to the sounds of the night,' they explained.

Sarika frowned. She had woken up one night to hear music. Aba-Aaji's house stood in a large compound, with trees lining the walls and a garden at the back. Their nearest neighbours were some distance away. Aba-Aaji talked to them sometimes from the terrace, shouting, 'How are you?' The neighbours called back polite things, and the wind brought scattered words, '...well...cold...going.' What did they mean? That their cold was gone or that they were going? The children soon discovered that the neighbours too had gone away for the summer. So where had the music come from?

'Tai,' Sachin said to Sarika, 'let's play!'

'Play with Piyush.'

'You play!'

'I am busy,' Sarika said.

Sarika was composing messages to Trisha in her head, trying to convey the horribleness of this vacation.

'What *can* Piyush do?' Sachin asked.

And yet, it was Piyush who brought excitement into their lives. He rushed in, an armful of books clutched to his chest.

'Look!' he said, face shining with delight. How could books make someone so happy, Sarika wondered, peering at them.

'Piyush...these are cookbooks!' Sarika said.

And they were, with pictures of food and titles like *Everyday Cooking*. On their covers steam rose enticingly and butter gleamed.

Piyush's face fell. Then, 'They're still books!' he grinned. He opened a book and was immediately lost in it.

'Read it aloud,' Sachin said. 'I want to hear too.'

Piyush obediently read out the name of the dish, the ingredients and how it was made. Sachin stopped him often to ask, 'What's that?' Sarika put away her messages to Trisha and tried to help. Sachin listened impatiently as she explained that mooli was *probably* radish, turmeric was the yellow stuff they had in the milk when they had colds and asafoetida was... 'No idea!' she admitted.

'Then how'll we make mooli parathas?' Sachin demanded.

'What?'

'You're no use,' Sachin told her as he raced away. 'Where's he gone?' Sarika wondered.

Sachin had gone to find Aba-Aaji. Sachin, who never noticed what he ate, because someone was usually stuffing food into his mouth while he stared at a screen, fingers clacking, had decided that he wanted mooli parathas.

'With butter,' Sarika heard him tell Aba. 'Melting. And a bowl of dahi.' Sachin, who didn't even like dahi!

'Yes, yes,' Aba said. He didn't seem upset at having his rest disturbed. 'We'll need to dig moolis from the garden first,' he announced.

'From the garden?' Piyush echoed.

'You grow *moolis*?' Sachin demanded. 'That's so cool!'

Aba handed Sachin a stubby thing to dig, pointed towards the moolis and sent him off. Sarika found him digging eagerly, sending lumps of mud flying. 'This mud...it's like chocolate!' he panted. Just wait till he finds his first worm, Sarika thought.

'Aah!' he said and her heart lurched. 'Mooli,' he announced.

The moolis were brown with mud and needed washing. Piyush ran to help and within minutes a splashing water battle began. Finally, they had gleaming white moolis and two wet brown boys. When they went away to change, Aba said, 'Start peeling, Sarika!'

'Me?'

'Don't you know how to peel?'

Sarika did. In a very clumsy, 'constantly dropping the peeler or the mooli' way. Sarika got very hot and bothered. Then Aaji came in, brisk as ever. 'Grate them,' she told Sarika.

There was no escape. Sarika sighed and began to grate. Hours later, she stopped because her fingers were tingling. To her horror, Sarika saw that she had grated her fingers too. Frantically she began to look in the pile of white gratings.

She only stopped when Aaji demanded, 'What are you doing?' Sarika backed away, her hand behind her back. It seemed as if they were going to have parathas with a scattering of fingers.

The parathas were delicious. As she ate them, Sarika wondered uneasily if the addition of finger flesh had made them so flaky. Sachin ate so many that Aba-Aaji were alarmed. 'Your stomach will hurt,' they warned.

'What if the others finish the parathas?' Sachin demanded.

'We'll make them again,' Aba promised.

'No, no,' Sachin said. 'We have so many other dishes to make!'

Overnight, Sachin and Piyush became friends. They spent hours together, Piyush reading from the cookbooks, Sachin listening.

'This looks interesting,' Piyush would say. 'Boring!' Sachin would decide. Or 'Too many ingredients!'

They raced through the books, finding recipes Sachin liked. Somehow, every recipe began with a visit to the garden and they became very familiar with it. It was warm there, with golden light glinting everywhere.

'What's that?' Piyush asked once, pointing to the roof. 'Solar panels,' Aaji said, 'to generate electricity.'

So the power wouldn't go off. Then why had Aai said...but Aaji was pointing to some leaves, dark veined and dancing on purple stalks, that she needed. Sarika plucked them, certain that Sachin had made a mistake this time. But the leaves—rolled, steamed, cut and fried—were delicious. Smacking her lips over their crisp taste, Sarika forgot her suspicions about the power.

One day Aba-Aaji had to go out. The minute they left, Piyush said, 'Let's make something!'

'But,' Sarika stammered. They'd never cooked without Aba-Aaji.

'We can do it,' Sachin said and Piyush nodded.

Sarika, not wanting to be a coward, bravely asked, 'What will we make?'

They riffled through the cookbooks, Piyush and Sarika pointing out recipes. 'No,' Sachin said. 'No, no!'

'*You* find the recipe then!' Sarika grumbled.

But Sachin had disappeared. He appeared just then, grinning hugely and waving a thin notebook. It was full of recipes in a tiny, cramped handwriting.

'Wonderful recipes!' Sachin sighed. 'Three-layered Cheese Rice! Three-flavoured pizza...'

They sounded terribly complicated but Sachin read them out as if he'd found a treasure.

'What are we making?' Piyush demanded.

Three-layered Rice or Three-fold Roti? Sachin couldn't decide.

Then Sarika asked, 'Who'll roll the rotis?' and that decided matters. Their rotis were uneven and often spouted ragged holes. Rice would be easier. Sarika soon discovered that *this* rice wasn't easy. They had to cook, then cool the rice. Then they rushed to the garden for tomatoes.

Sachin was frowning over the recipe. 'Terrible handwriting,' Sarika said, trying to read. '*Great* tomatoes?' she laughed.

'Grate tomatoes,' Sachin said. Sarika stopped laughing when the tomatoes slithered and slid away. 'Use the blender,' she said. 'But...the recipe?' Piyush wondered.

'It'll be okay,' she said. It was. 'You have good ideas, Tai!' Sachin sounded surprised. Sarika felt a flicker of annoyance till she realized that she was surprised at herself too. And at Sachin's fearless cooking, at Piyush's tireless helping. They worked well together, she thought, as they slid the rice into the oven.

Aba-Aaji had trained them well. They cleaned the counters and washed the dishes while they watched the oven. When it pinged, they raced to pull the dish out. A wonderful smell filled the kitchen.

'Cheese!' Piyush moaned.

'Coriander!'

'Wait,' Sachin said, 'turn!' Piyush looked surprised but obediently turned on the spot.

'What are you doing?' Sachin demanded.

'You said turn,' Piyush explained.

'Turn,' Sarika read from the book.

'See?'

'Wait!' Sarika said. '*We* don't turn, turn the rice onto a plate!'

'What terrible instructions!' Sachin said while Piyush muttered, 'Asking me to turn!'

Sarika was giggling as she ran to find a pen. She bumped into Aba-Aaji, who asked, 'Where are you going?'

The giggling must have weakened her for she said at once, 'To get a pen...to correct a recipe!' They stared and she explained, 'It's a recipe in a little book and the instructions are terrible...'

Aba ran into the kitchen shouting, 'What have you done?' Then he stopped. 'My Three-layered Cheese Rice,' he muttered.

'Not yours,' Piyush corrected. '*For* you!'

Aba pointed to the book in Sarika's hand, 'That's my book and...'

'Did you...are these your recipes?' Sarika asked.

'Did you invent them?' Piyush was more direct.

Aba nodded.

There was a stunned silence. 'Your Aba,' Aaji told them, 'likes creating new recipes more than reading cookbooks!'

'But I don't have the courage to try them out,' Aba told them.

'They are brilliant!'

Aba turned eagerly to Sachin. 'Really?'

'Yes,' Sachin nodded.

'Do you think people will like them?' Aba wondered.

Aaji thumped plates on the table and said, 'Let's find out!'

Aba hung back. 'People,' he said again. '*Other* people!'

Sarika understood at once. 'Yes,' she said. 'If I had my phone, I would've taken a picture for Instagr...'

A phone was pushed into her hand. She stared at it.

'It's mine,' Aba said. So, they had phones connected to the Internet, phones that could have Instagram set up. In silence, Sarika did just that. She typed the recipe, making changes as she wrote, checked the phone again and again, reading comments out to Aba. But when she tried to get him to do anything, he said the screen was too small.

'You need an iPad,' Sachin said. And immediately, one appeared. So, that was the music she had heard!

'How?' Sachin asked.

'Why?' Sarika asked. Why had they said they had no Wi-Fi and no power? Why had they said the TV didn't work?

'Without your phones and books we hoped you'd look up,' Aba-Aaji said, 'see us, talk to us!' 'We wanted that,' Aba said. Aaji nodded.

The children knew a moment of shame. Then Piyush asked, 'What will we make next?' and the awkward moment was lost.

The next few days the children tried out many new recipes. Sarika tried to train Aba to click photos and post the recipes. But he was always running away to invent new recipes to show Sachin, who only had to hear a recipe to know if it would work. He said he saw the recipe in his mind. Just like Sarika knew which photos to post and Piyush knew just how he could help.

There was no time to miss home or her phone. So when Aai came to Nagpur to take them home, and handed Sarika her phone, she stared. There were dozens of messages from Trisha, asking about the vacation.

Sarika thought of all she'd seen when she looked up from her phone—the garden and Aaji's brisk bossiness, Piyush's smile, Sachin's all-seeing eye, and Aba's creativity. She was weighed by the knowledge of how much she would miss them and tears swam in her eyes.

She sniffed, swallowed, then typed, 'Just a typical vacation with the grandparents!'

Dance, Nani, Dance!

DEEPA AGARWAL

That December afternoon, Navya was walking on air as she headed home from the bus stop with her older brother Vivaan. It was one of those relatively less polluted Delhi days and the buttery sunshine made their neighbour's yellow chrysanthemums look cheerier than ever.

Her eyes opened wide when Ma opened the door instead of Mamta.

'Ma!' Vivaan exclaimed behind her. 'You never mentioned you were going to take leave today?'

'Oh, I just decided to come home early,' Ma said with a faint smile.

Twelve-year-old Navya was thrilled. It almost felt as if Ma had sensed that Navya had big news which she was dying to share. News that wouldn't keep till the evening. But something in her mother's expression made her uneasy—as if everything was not okay.

'Cool!' Vivaan grinned, putting down his school bag. At fifteen, his voice had turned quite bass, and he towered over his skinny younger sister. Navya hoped that she too would grow tall like him. He turned to her, 'What are you waiting for? Tell Ma!'

Ma raised her eyebrows questioningly. 'Ma, our team won the first prize in the debating competition.' Navya's eyes gleamed with excitement.

'Brilliant!' Ma hugged her tightly. 'I'm so proud of you, dear. All your hard work has paid off!'

Navya drew in a deep, satisfied breath. 'Now come and have your lunch,' Ma said. 'There's gajar ka halwa for dessert.'

Her favourite dessert! It felt like a reward. Navya was scooping up the last bit of the cardamom-flavoured halwa from her bowl when Vivaan stood up. 'I'm off to my coaching class,' he said.

The preoccupied look Navya had noticed returned to Ma's face. 'Wait a minute,' she said. 'There's something I want to tell both of you.'

A twinge of anxiety twisted Navya's stomach. Was something wrong?

'Nani's coming for a visit,' Ma said.

'Nani's coming?' Navya burst out happily. She loved her grandmother and always looked forward to her visits.

'Great!' Vivaan's face lit up too.

'Yes,' Ma continued. 'But it's different this time. She's going to move in with us permanently.'

'Oh...' Navya froze. Her grandmother had always been very independent and insisted on living alone. 'Is-is something wrong?'

Ma sighed. 'She's developed some health problems...and we feel it's not safe for her to live alone,' she kept her eyes fixed on the table.

Vivaan cleared his throat. 'I'm sorry to hear that,' he said softly. 'What's wrong with her?

'Just old-age issues.' Ma's voice had a sad note.

'Oh...' Vivaan's face fell. After a pause, he said, 'Ma, I'd better leave, or I'll be late.'

Ma nodded distractedly. Navya wanted to get up too, but she got the feeling that Ma wanted to say something more. And the moment the door closed behind Vivaan, Ma began, 'Navya, she will share your room as usual. This is why I came back early—to make arrangements. She'll be here tomorrow...I know this is a bit sudden, but your father and I have been discussing it for some time and we felt it was better not to delay any more.'

It took a while for Ma's words to sink in. Nani always shared Navya's room when she came on visits. But that was different. Navya's heart plunged when she realized what it meant.

'I know it'll be a big adjustment for you, dear,' Ma squeezed her arm. 'But as of now it would be impossible for us to move into a bigger house.'

Navya gulped. 'It's all right, Ma,' she said bravely. 'Don't worry, I'll adjust.'

Ma sighed and got to her feet. 'We'd better get cracking.'

In a daze Navya helped Ma make space in her room—clear all the clutter, remove extra clothes from her closet to make space for Nani's, put away some of her stuffed toys that were all over the place. The news was so sudden. Her throat felt tight as she thought how much she loved having her room to herself. It was her personal space, her refuge when she wanted to be alone. Where she rehearsed her debates, shot the silly, fun videos she liked to make. She adored her grandmother, and it felt a bit mean, but the thought of sharing her room permanently was hard to accept.

Nani arrived the next day—bag and baggage. There was plenty of it. Two large suitcases and miscellaneous stuff. Steel containers with Navya's favourite besan laddoos, jars of pickle and freshly picked guavas from the tree in her house.

'Ah...Navya!' she beamed as she hugged her. 'But...who's this boy?'

Ma laughed. 'I know, Vivaan has changed a lot since you last saw him.'

'Vivaan...what a big boy you are now,' Nani gave him a puzzled smile. 'Come on, you two. Try the laddoos...and the guavas.'

Navya bit into a laddoo. It was too sweet, she thought. But she couldn't hurt Nani's feelings, so she said, 'As yummy as ever, Nani!'

'Nani looks fine to me,' Vivaan whispered, his mouth full of laddoo.

'She does,' Navya agreed. It was true. Nani looked just the way she always had. Her eyes were as bright, her cheeks as plump and her voice as loud and jolly.

They helped her unpack and arranged all her things. 'Navya,' Nani said suddenly. 'I hope you'll enjoy having me as a roommate.'

'Of course, Nani!' Navya hoped she sounded convincing. She would not upset her grandmother for the world, but oh...how she would miss her privacy!

'Well, you'll just have to get used to it,' her friend Vinnie said, when she told her in school. 'You can come and practise your debates in my house, whenever you want.'

'Thanks,' Navya said. But it only cheered her up slightly. It would not be the same as practising in her own room.

A week went by. Navya was trying hard to adjust. The weather turned colder, and Nani wanted the heater on all the time. It was suffocating. She got up at least three times in the night to use the loo, which woke Navya up—she was a light sleeper. And she kept dispensing advice on Navya's homework, her clothes, her appearance.

Then one afternoon, when they got home, Mamta opened the door with a broad smile on her face. Navya was astonished to hear a Bollywood number blaring in the drawing room. And even more astonished to see Nani gyrating to the music.

She stopped when Navya and Vivaan entered. 'What do you think of my moves?' she asked. 'Mamta said I should shake my hips more.'

Navya turned to meet her brother's horrified gaze. She wanted to give Mamta a piece of her mind. But she had retreated to the kitchen to bring out lunch.

'Er...you're doing well, Nani,' she said awkwardly. 'But shall we have lunch now?'

'Of course, my dear,' Nani agreed, turning off the music.

As they tucked into kadhi and rice, Nani said, 'You must be wondering why I was dancing.'

'Oh...I guess you were trying to pass your time,' Vivaan volunteered.

Nani laughed loudly. 'It's more than that. You know I love to dance.'

Don't I? Navya thought. She recalled Nani performing at her cousin's wedding and how embarrassed she had felt because Nani had chosen a rather romantic song to dance to. Not at all suitable for a person her age.

Aloud she said, 'Um...yes.'

'Well, I discovered that there is a TV competition happening—just for seniors. I thought it would be a good idea to try my luck.' Nani's eyes twinkled merrily.

Navya suppressed the gasp that was bursting out of her throat, but Vivaan couldn't.

'Impressed, aren't you?' Nani smiled mischievously. 'I thought, why not? But please keep it a secret from your mother. I don't want her to feel disappointed if I don't clear the audition.'

Navya swallowed hard. She exchanged a quick glance with Vivaan. He had gone red. She could almost read the thought going through his mind. *This can't be happening!*

'But Nani...' she said quickly. 'I hope it's okay...I mean with your health problems and all. You shouldn't overexert.'

'Health problems? I may be seventy-six, but I walk four kilometres every morning,' Nani said with a frown.

'True...' Navya had to concede. Then she rose hastily, 'Uh-uh...I have a lot of homework to complete.'

Vivaan made his escape too. But as Navya was entering her room, Nani called out, 'When you're done, I'd like your thoughts on the second dance I'm preparing. I don't have too much faith in Mamta's judgement.'

'Okay, Nani,' Navya said dispiritedly. The idea didn't appeal to her at all, but it would have been too awful to say, 'No, I can't'.

So, every afternoon after completing her homework, she would patiently watch her grandmother perform. After a couple of days, she couldn't help suggesting gently, 'Nani, why don't you choose another song?'

'Why? Am I not doing justice to "*Chhaiyan chhaiyan*"? I've studied each and every one of Malaika Arora's moves.'

Navya cast about frantically in her mind. 'It's not that. It's just that I felt...'

'Felt what? That I'm too old for this song?' Nani glared at her.

'No, no, Nani! I-I thought since you're so graceful...something like "*Mohe panghat pe Nandlal*"...' Navya was impressed by her own quick thinking.

Nani beamed. 'You are a smart girl. Actually, I have danced to that number, so I have my steps pat. Okay, find it on the phone.'

When Nani began swaying to the song, however, Navya cursed herself for suggesting it. Nani's moves were too-too filmi and her expressions so embarrassingly coy.

Worse, keeping this a secret from her mother felt like she was carrying a big rock on her back. How she wished that the audition day would arrive, and it would all be over! The thought shamed her, but she fervently hoped that Nani would not be selected. That way they would be spared the mortification of seeing her perform on TV with millions of people watching.

Two stress-laden weeks dragged by. 'All well?' Vinnie asked in school one day. 'You've been looking so anxious. Remember, I told you you're most welcome to come over to my place to do your stuff.'

Navya took a deep breath. 'You won't believe what I'm going to tell you. Nani's preparing to take part in a TV dance competition for seniors.'

Vinnie burst into peals of laughter. Then she wiped her eyes and said, 'Sorry, I didn't mean to make fun. But wow! I think your Nani's very cool. What spirit!'

'Too much of it,' Navya huffed. 'If only she'd behave like a grandmother.'

'Come on, Navya,' Vinnie said. 'What's wrong with a grandmother dancing? You should be proud of her for debunking a stereotype.'

Navya blinked. This is exactly what she had argued about in her last debate. Debunking stereotypes. But it was so hard to accept when it was your own grandmother dancing in a competition!

Vinnie's remark really made her think, however. All the way home in the bus her thoughts were in turmoil. And eventually, she had to grudgingly admit that she should be proud of Nani for being so feisty.

On their way home from the bus stop, Vivaan asked, 'Will Nani be practising again this afternoon?'

'You know that's her afternoon routine.' Navya scowled.

'Yeah...but can't you head her off today? Amar and Tarun are coming over.' He chewed his lower lip. 'It'll be a little awkward.'

Navya didn't know what to say. She could understand Vivaan's position, but these rehearsals were so important for Nani. She put her heart and soul into them.

'All right,' she said reluctantly. 'Maybe I'll ask her to make besan laddoos.'

'Thanks, Navs!' Vivaan exclaimed joyfully. 'You're the best.'

Navya didn't feel that she was the best. She felt like a lowlife when she told Nani, 'Can we make some besan laddoos today? We've eaten up the ones you brought.' Then as a pang of guilt stabbed her, she added, 'But you'll miss your practice.'

'What does one day matter? I'll make up tomorrow.' Nani's warm smile made Navya feel worse.

The ingredients were assembled. Besan, ghee, sugar, cardamom. 'Umm...' Nani said, knitting her brow. 'Now to measure them... but...I can't remember how much of each I use.'

Navya stared at Nani. She looked so confused that Navya's heart thumped hard. Nani always had the ingredients at her fingertips.

'Oh...that's no problem,' she said quickly. 'I'll get a recipe from the Internet.'

The laddoos turned out perfect. But a nagging apprehension took hold of Navya. She hoped there was nothing seriously wrong with Nani.

Her mood felt different when she watched Nani rehearsing next day—less irritated, more supportive. When Nani finished a number, she cried out, clapping spontaneously, 'You're really doing great, Nani!' Nani *was* really good. How could she have been so opposed to this idea?

At last, the audition day arrived. Luckily, Nani had got an afternoon slot. When they finished lunch, Navya said, 'Come on, Nani, let's get ready.'

'Ready for what?' Nani asked, wrinkling her brow.

Navya's mouth dropped open. 'For your audition!' she said.

'Audition?' Nani seemed even more bewildered.

'For the dance competition. Have you forgotten?'

Nani looked so blank that Navya's heart plunged. 'Come on, Nani,' she said frantically. 'Get ready. We'll be late. You've been practising so hard.'

'Practising...I've been practising...to which song?' Nani asked hesitantly.

'So many of them. I'll tell you on the way.'

Nani looked quite stunning, Navya thought, in a bright pink sari with a broad golden border and matching jewellery. As they headed off in the taxi, she was humming '*Mohe panghat pe Nandlal*'. Her colourful bangles tinkled as she rehearsed her hand movements. Navya was praying with all her heart, please god, let Nani make it.

When they returned, they found that Ma was back from the office. 'Where were you?' she asked, frowning.

'Congratulate me, my dear,' Nani said pertly, planting a kiss on her cheek. 'I have cleared the audition for the *Naache Nani, Naache Dadi* competition on TV. All thanks to our darling Navya. You can't imagine what a wonderful support she has been.'

Navya flushed a deep red when Nani said this. Did she really deserve this praise?

'TV competition!' Ma exclaimed, turning from Nani to Navya. 'What's all this?'

The whole story was told, about the secret preparations and Navya's role. Ma's eyes teared up when they finished. 'I'm so proud of both of you,' she whispered.

'Wow, Nani, congrats!' Vivaan was impressed too.

When Nani went to change out of her dance outfit, Navya burst out, 'Ma, Nani was practising every day, but she forgot all about the competition today. What's wrong with her?'

Ma went silent. Then she sighed deeply. 'I didn't want to make you kids anxious but...the doctor's diagnosed Alzheimer's.'

'Oh, Ma.' Navya could not control her tears.

'Yes...' Ma brushed at her eyes. 'But with our love and support...she can lead a comfortable life.' She choked up.

'I'll do everything I can,' Navya cried. 'She's the most amazing Nani anyone could have.'

'So will I,' Vivaan added determinedly. 'She *is* truly amazing!'

Something Fishy in the Neighbourhood

SAYANTAN GHOSH

Sunny's Calcutta was made of wet monsoon fields, of bright nights when the full moon reflected on the surface of the local pond, of endless street cricket during summer holidays. When he wasn't made to sit and study by his mother, he was always out in the open—feeding the grey cat who lived in Mr Sahni's garage, climbing the mango tree that stood between their house and the Government High School, or just lying on their terrace, staring at the sky, and counting the number of stars which were visible that day. Even when his friends were busy, Sunny was busy adventuring on his own.

Among all the things that kept his mind occupied, the one that fascinated him most was that old, abandoned house surrounded by a rickety wall in their neighbourhood, which all the adults avoided passing by after sunset.

Children were prohibited from going that way even during the day. People used to say that an old man, Mr Mitter, once lived there happily with his loving wife and a Labrador called Bagha. They celebrated festivals with their neighbours, invited guests over for lunches, joyfully participated in the Durga Puja organized by the Youth Club every year.

They didn't have any children or close relatives, so they always made it a point to mingle with everyone. When Bagha died, both Mr and Mrs Mitter were heartbroken and were often seen sitting near the grave where they had buried Bagha in their garden and lamenting. And once Mrs Mitter passed away a few years later, the man stopped coming out of the house altogether. Spending his final years in solitude, he died without anyone noticing. It was almost three days before a foul smell attracted the attention of a local milkman one morning. In the months that followed, some claimed they saw a shadow at the window of the empty house watching passers-by on the road. One night, an elderly lady who used to beg for a living was sleeping under a neem tree facing the house. She was inconsolable the next morning and ran around the locality shouting the words, 'Those scaly hands won't spare anyone! Those scaly hands won't spare anyone!' She was never seen again in the neighbourhood. Ever since then, the house had remained locked up.

But Sunny was weirdly drawn to that house. He had heard someone say that in his last years, all that the old man did to spend his time, was read. He had turned a part of the ground floor into a mini library. There were oakwood shelves that lined the walls of the room. The shelves were filled with books from all around the world. All Sunny ever wanted was to go inside just one time and get a glimpse of the old man's book collection. Because, it was in the world of stories where Sunny felt most at home. There was a bookshop next to the High School near Sunny's home where he went every day and read all the books that he could find there. If there was no new book available, then he would just pick up something he may have already read before and reread it. He could get tired of other people, but never of reading, never of books.

It's not that he hadn't attempted to enter the premises. A couple of times he had dared to cross the wall when the sun was still up, tiptoe through the garden, and tried to push open the main door. But the door was so tightly shut that he could never push it open.

Just when he was about to give up hope, his best buddy Polo told him, 'You know, it's true the door remains closed all day but it automatically opens if someone goes there at night.'

That surprised Sunny. 'How do you know this?'

Polo said, 'Abhi and his friends had discovered this one day when they had sneaked in for fun. He told me.' Abhi was Polo's elder brother.

That was all the motivation Sunny needed. He said to Polo, 'You're going to come with me. Don't say no!'

Polo instantly started shaking his head and said, 'That's not happening. You can do what you want, but I'm not risking my life for another stupid expedition of yours. Have you forgotten how I nearly broke my nose last year when you wanted to investigate who steals puppies from our colony at night?'

'That's just because you couldn't run fast. Who had asked you to fall down in the middle of the road?'

Polo replied with embarrassment, 'I was just frightened and slipped.'

'But we found the culprit. That night guard would have kept stealing and selling those innocent puppies if we hadn't caught him red-handed.'

'Yes, but...'

Before Polo could complete his sentence Sunny said, 'You can have my SG cricket bat for an entire week if you come with me.'

After that Polo didn't need too much convincing.

It was a Saturday in December, and most families were spending a cosy evening, gathered around their television. Sunny told his parents he had to go to Polo's house to collect a textbook. Since the boys were forever running to and from each others' houses, they hardly paid him any attention. Polo told his parents the same lie.

They met in front of the dreaded Mitter house at 7 p.m. It was particularly quiet all around or maybe it was the night playing tricks with Sunny's mind. The moon was nothing but a sliver in the sky, and a streetlight was flickering repeatedly about twenty yards from the house. A cycle rickshaw puller went past them, and they waited till he had disappeared in the mist. Very quietly, they climbed the wall and walked closer towards the wooden main door which guarded the house all day. But as soon as Sunny touched the handle, the door opened on its own. As though an invisible force was inviting them inside.

Polo was about to scream when Sunny put his palm on Polo's mouth. 'Don't make a sound, Polo,' he said. They were both scared, but Sunny didn't want to miss this golden opportunity he may never get again. As they entered, they could smell something strange. Like something was rotting inside the house for years. Sunny switched on his torch.

The light from the torch fell on the dusty yet beautiful bookshelves, with rows and rows of rare and exquisite books kept on them. Sunny's fears vanished. They were arranged alphabetically, as though a deft librarian had been at work. Sunny reached out and pulled out a handsome hardbound copy of *Treasure Island* by Robert Louis Stevenson. Right on cue, Polo let off a blood-curdling yell for help.

Polo was frozen like an ice statue. His face had lost colour, and he was pointing towards the hallway which was so dark that Sunny had no idea what had frightened Polo so much. Sunny swung the torchlight in the direction of Polo's index finger. He saw a hand. It was longer than a regular human hand, and it was covered in scales. Like a fish. When he could look away from the hand, he noticed two red eyes hovering above the hand. They were burning bright and looking straight at the two of them. Even from that distance, Sunny could tell that the figure was at least eight feet tall.

Without wasting another second, he grabbed Polo's arm and ran for the door. Sprinting across the garden as they were climbing the outer wall, both of them heard a hair-raising laugh coming from inside the house. They didn't stop running until they had reached their respective homes. When Sunny entered his room panting, he realized that the copy of *Treasure Island* he had taken out from the shelf was still in his hand.

Sunny didn't step out of his room the rest of the evening and was too afraid to switch off the lights and go to sleep alone that night. Around 11 p.m., he went to his grandfather's room and knocked on the door. Usually, his grandfather would be reading or writing at his desk at this hour. When his grandfather opened the door, Sunny said, 'Dadu, can I sleep in your room tonight?' His grandfather said, 'Sure, Sunny. Is everything all right?' Sunny nodded and went inside the room.

That night, his sleep was broken by the sound of footsteps around the bed where Sunny and his Dadu were asleep. Sunny looked at the wall clock and saw that it was 3:30 a.m.

in the morning. He rubbed his eyes and tried to clear his vision to check what was causing the disturbance. What he saw sent a chill down his spine. Those same red eyes, and an eight-foot-tall figure standing in one corner of the room. The scaly hands were raised in Sunny's direction as if they were trying to reach him.

Sunny tried his best to scream, but the only word that came out of his mouth was, 'DADU!'

That was enough for his grandfather, who was anyway a light sleeper, to wake up. Dadu quickly switched on the light and asked Sunny what was the matter. This time Sunny didn't hesitate and recounted the whole story about their visit to the haunted home in their neighbourhood and the scaly hands which had now followed him home. Dadu listened to Sunny with a serious face. He was expecting Dadu to give him a scolding. He knew Dadu wouldn't ground him because he never stopped Sunny from exploring the outdoors. But Dadu said reassuringly, 'It's a little far-fetched, but I believe you, son. I know you never lie.' That gave Sunny a lot of strength and confidence. Then

Dadu asked him to go back to sleep, adding, 'Let's keep the light on tonight. Tomorrow morning, we'll go to that house together.'

The rest of the night passed peacefully.

Next morning, Sunny and Dadu made their way to the house. Dadu inspected it from the outside for some time and then walked to the back. There was something distinctly odd about the house, for sure. But what was it? Dadu stopped at a window at the back of the house. He sniffed the air. Sunny did too, and he caught hold of Dadu's hand hard. It was the same rotten smell from last night! They had to get out of there. Fast.

'Come with me,' he said to Sunny. They walked to a local teashop which was a few buildings away and sat down on a shaky bench. Dadu made small talk with the owner of the teashop for a while, and then asked him about the house. The man told them the same story of the old man and his family which was popular in the locality. With one additional piece of information. 'That old fellow, all he loved doing was reading books and eating fish every day of the week. Each morning, I would see the local fish seller walking towards his house with a basket full of fresh fish.' It was easy for Dadu to join the dots after that.

That afternoon, Dadu sat Sunny down to share some of his thoughts with him.

'You have made a mistake, my dear boy. You should have never gone to that house because although no one lives there, it is still someone's private property. But that isn't your biggest mistake. You took something from there that doesn't belong to you. Do you know what that is called?'

Sunny lowered his head and murmured, 'I know. Stealing. But I didn't mean to steal the book. When I ran, I forgot that it was in my hand.'

'I know,' Dadu said. 'And that is why tonight we must return the book where it belongs.' Sunny couldn't believe his ears. 'Do you mean... we will go back to that house?'

Dadu smiled and kept his hand on Sunny's shoulder. 'Don't worry, I'll be there with you.' Before they went to the house, Dadu told Sunny that they had another job to do. They took a rickshaw to the Adarsha Hindu Hotel near the station which was famous for its fish curry. At the restaurant, Dadu said to the man at the counter, 'Pack me a plate of your best fish curry, and make sure you give me the biggest piece!'

From there, the rickshaw dropped them in front of the cursed house. Sunny was hanging on tight to *Treasure Island.*

Dadu held Sunny's trembling hand and walked inside from the back where the wall was broken. 'We are doing what's right, so there's absolutely nothing to fear,' he said to his grandson. Sunny was relieved to hear it.

The main door opened on its own like the previous night. Dadu took out his torch and they headed straight for the room with the bookshelves. 'Just keep looking ahead, don't turn your head,' Dadu told Sunny. Once in the room, Dadu opened the packet and brought out the delicious fish curry from it. He placed it on a small table which stood in the centre of the room. 'Now put the book back exactly where you had taken it from,' he told Sunny.

As soon as the Stevenson novel was back where it belonged, Sunny could hear his grandfather's booming voice behind him.

'You spirit of the house, I know you are upset because my grandson took your book by mistake. He has come to return it and apologize to you. And for all your troubles, we have brought you your favourite food as a gift. I know you haven't had your beloved fish curry in many years. Eat to your heart's content and forgive my grandson. I request you not to follow him and come back to our house again.'

They waited for a few seconds before Sunny noticed those red eyes again. The figure's hands and legs, all covered in slimy scales, were visible too. Only this time, there was also a smile under the eyes that could be clearly seen.

As Sunny and Dadu were walking out of the house, they heard a chomping sound behind them. Someone was greatly enjoying a long due meal.

From that day on, sunlight returned to the interiors of the haunted house. The main door remained open all day, the foul smell was all but gone. And anyone could visit the room with the bookshelves and read any book they wanted to. No one was there to stop them anymore.

At first, like everyone else in the locality, even Sunny was curious to know how this change came about. But one afternoon when he was playing with marbles, he saw Dadu going towards the Mitter house. He wouldn't have bothered to take a second look, since it wasn't uncommon for Dadu to go out on walks at odd hours, if he hadn't spotted that familiar packet from Adarsha Hindu Hotel in his hand. He immediately knew what was inside—a portion of mouth-watering fish curry. It wasn't a mystery to Sunny any longer how the cursed home became a local library for the young and the old alike. Only one thing was prohibited though. The books were never to be taken outside those walls.

Talking to Ants

ASHOK BANKER

Neel was in the back garden when he saw the ants spelling out letters.

Only moments earlier, they had all sat down to lunch at Nani's old dining table and Papa had served them kathal curry, made 'exactly as per Nani's own recipe'. The raw jackfruit in the curry was from Nani's tree in her backyard.

It had all been too much for Neel, bringing back sweet and painful memories, and he had excused himself from the table. He came to the back garden to sit on this swing, where he was now rocking back and forth aimlessly. The back and forth motion of the swing was hypnotic, not quite enough to forget the terrible truth, but enough to dull the sharp prick of reality just a little. It was soothing, though he had to fight to keep out the memories of all the times he had spent on this same swing with Nani.

That was when he happened to look down and see the ants.

They were black ants.

Neel was used to seeing black ants here. The sweet sticky juice of fallen jackfruit always attracted them.

Once Mama had told Nani she should use pest control to get rid of them. Nani had made that nasal sound she made when something offended her and said that black ants were auspicious.

Neel had listened and had had mixed feelings.

When Neel had been younger and visited Bangalore during his summer vacations, he would get scared of the ants. He would worry they might bite him and would always make sure to keep his feet up on the swing, like he was doing now.

Even after he grew out of it, he would still pause at the back door, run like mad to the swing and throw himself on top of it, as if afraid that the ants would catch him and eat him up alive!

Nani used to tease him, walking her fingers up his bare feet to his knees, chanting 'Chinti chori! Chinti chori!' in her cracked voice.

He would giggle and wriggle and tell her to stop.

It was one of the many little things he missed.

What were these ants up to today?

Neel watched them swarming across the back garden. The garden looked sadly neglected. After years of Nani's loving care and daily attention, it had been untended for over three months.

Her lovely rose bushes were all bare and thorny, the marigolds wilted, a carpet of discarded petals below, as if it had been weeping orange tears, even her bougainvillea looking frail and dusty.

Everything looked different. The ants seemed lost and confused, milling about the garden like people queueing up in an endless line. If Nani was here, she would have said something funny, like maybe they're queueing up for Aadhaar cards.

Neel knew the thought of ants queueing up for their Aadhaar cards was funny but couldn't bring himself to smile. He was just too sad.

He frowned down at the ants, wondering what was wrong with *them*?

The ants were not moving.

Instead of swarming to and fro as they always did, they were standing curiously still, a large black cluster on the thinning, unwatered grass through which the ground peeped out in bare patches. It reminded Neel of the growing bald spot on the back of Papa's head. The lovely, lush lawn that Nani had maintained so lovingly was half-dead. It was another painful reminder of her absence.

Why weren't the ants moving, Neel wondered.

It seemed as if they were all gathered together, waiting and watching.

Waiting for what?

Watching what?

A spidery tingle started in the soles of his feet, rising up his ankles.

He looked down to check, just in case, but there were no ants on him.

Still, the feeling was so strong, he wriggled a little on the swing. It creaked softly as it swayed.

The old nylon ropes were almost worn smooth where he held them; where Nani's creased palms must have held them so many times. He held them tighter, imagining they were still warm from her grip.

The crow that sat on Nani's roof and cawed endlessly was mercifully absent. The back garden was quiet except for the sound of traffic.

The ants began to move.

Not randomly as they always did, but purposefully, forming a pattern, like soldiers lined up in ranks, marching in step, turning and moving as one.

Neel had read somewhere—or perhaps Nani had read it and told him—that human beings and ants were the only two species on the planet that waged war. Neel had asked her what it meant. Nani had thought about it a long time, swinging on this swing with Neel beside her, then finally said that she thought it meant that they had the capacity for organization, and could work together to achieve a common goal. She pointed out that ants could undertake complex engineering tasks that required a high degree of skill, such as building a bridge of leaves and twigs to cross a small stream. Who knew what amazing things they could do when motivated?

The ants were forming a pattern now.

Neel watched them, fascinated. He tried to make out the shapes in their pattern, the way one might look for dragons and dinosaurs in the shapes of clouds.

He lay down on the swing. If Neel lay on it sideways, he could almost fit. He lay sideways now, head and feet dangling over the sides, and watched the ants at work.

They were moving quite fast now, the orderly rows and lines rippling and moving like marching bands across a football stadium.

He squinted, turning his head this way then that, trying to see sense in the pattern.

On impulse, he stood up on the swing, holding the nylon ropes for support, and tried to make it stand still.

Even before it came completely to a stop, he saw the letters emerge.

The ants were forming letters and the letters spelled words.

Neel stared in astonishment as the words appeared magically on the ground of Nani's back garden.

HELLO NEEL

I MISS YOU LITTLE BOO

Neel almost fell off the swing.

He sat down heavily, only his grip on the ropes keeping him from falling right off. His heart was thudding. His breathing had quickened.

He couldn't believe what he was seeing.

Little Boo.

Neel's first word when he spoke as an infant was 'Boo'. Only his parents, siblings and Nana and Nani had known that. Even his father's parents, Neel's Dada and Dadi, didn't know that because they lived in the US and Neel only spoke to them over Facetime occasionally; he had met them only once, and they were not close.

But Nani had known that.

And in moments of affection, only Nani had called him, privately, 'Little Boo'. Not even Mama or Papa knew that.

He stared at the words the ants had spelled out, closed his eyes, shook his head vigorously, then opened them again.

The words were still there.

After a very long pause, during which Neel felt emotions he couldn't have described or named, he finally said, in a tear-choked voice, 'Nani?'

The ants rippled, their ranks moving.

They were faster the second time.

New words formed and when they were done, the message read:

HELLO LITTLE BOO

BE KIND TO YOURSELF

REMEMBER, DEAR BOY, ONE SEASON ENDS ONLY TO GIVE WAY TO THE NEXT

Neel stared at the words, trying to digest their meaning.

Finally, he said, quietly, as if to himself, 'How are you, Nani?'

The ants rippled.

LITTLE BOO I AM WELL AND WATCHING OVER YOU

Then, a smaller group formed:

HOW ARE YOU BETA

Neel looked around, hardly able to believe this was really happening. The crow had returned and was squatting on the roof of the cottage but for once, he wasn't squawking.

'I miss you, Nani,' Neel said.

OH BETA

I AM SORRY

IN TIME YOU WILL FEEL BETTER

I PROMISE

Neel was about to ask another question when the crow on the roof of the cottage cawed harshly.

'Neel?' said a voice.

For a moment, Neel almost thought the voice was Nani's, that he would turn around and see her smiling face again, creased with more lines than he could count.

But it was only Mama. She was holding a plate.

'You didn't eat your lunch. I brought you a sandwich.'

Neel looked down at the ants, wondering if Mama had noticed them yet. What would she think of the message they had spelled out.

But the ground was clear of letters and words now. Only the dirt patches and sparse, half-dead grass was visible. And a number of ants clustered around the fallen pieces of sticky, gooey jackfruit, the same as always.

On the roof, the crow cawed again and flew away.

* * *

The next day, Neel's parents got the bright idea that Neel needed cheering up. They dragged him off to some Children's Exhibition. It was a massive thing, hundreds of stalls selling toys and books and all sorts of products for kids.

The place was packed with crowds because of the holiday weekend, mostly little kids yelling and screaming, some older teens browsing fantasy novels about evil unicorns and warring aliens, and Neel couldn't think of anything less cheering.

The crowds and the noise made him feel even more alone and lonely.

He wished he could be back home, so he could sit on the swing in the back garden and see if the ants were still there.

After a night's sleep, he couldn't believe it had really happened.

Surely it had only been a daydream? Maybe he had fallen asleep lying on the swing. It had happened before.

But Sarana and Anmol wanted to see the latest Marvel movie, and Papa and Mama thought it would be a good thing for Neel too. So they had dragged him to the multiplex for a lunch he didn't feel like eating and a movie he didn't feel like seeing. He showed his resentment by speaking only in grunts all day.

By the time they got home, it was dark and he had to go straight to bed. He put his face to the closed bedroom window, trying to look down into the back garden. The glass felt cold against his pressed nose. The garden was too dark to see anything. He wondered if ants even came out in the night. Probably not.

The next morning, he was the first one up at the crack of dawn and tiptoed down the stairs, careful not to wake anyone.

In his pajamas and chappals, Neel went out to the swing. It was cold and his breath misted a little as he breathed out.

He paused at the back door out of old habit.

There were no ants visible.

He felt disappointed. Maybe it *had* been just a daydream then?

Still, he couldn't bring himself to just go back to bed.

The ground was wreathed in fog, making it impossible to see the grass clearly.

If there were ants, he couldn't see them.

Still, as he walked across the denuded lawn, he stepped carefully, hoping he wasn't squishing any ants under his rubber chappals.

He sat on the swing and looked around.

He could see the back door but the top of the roof was lost in the white haze and the back wall of the garden, only fifteen or twenty feet away, was invisible.

After waiting for several minutes he began to feel cold and sleepy and more than a little foolish.

He lay down on the swing, curling up into a ball. The rocking motion lulled him: he hadn't slept much last night and sleep came easily now.

As he drifted off, he imagined feeling Nani bending over him as he slept, gently caressing his forehead, tousling his hair.

He could almost smell the scents of her last chore on her hands: the pungent smell of ground spices, or the fragrance of ripe mangoes freshly cut, or the woody smell of the old books she lovingly read and reread over and over.

'Why am I still here, Nani?' he mumbled.

The rest of the thought was completed only in his mind as he slipped into the arms of Morpheus.

We are all still here: Papa, Mama, Anmol, Sarana, and me.

Your house is still here.

Even the old crow on the roof is still here.

But you are gone forever, Nani.

I don't want to be here.

I don't like the world without you, Nani.

I feel cold and lonely, lost and alone.

Nobody understands me like you do.

I know Papa and Mama love me but they are too busy with their own lives and careers.

Anmol and Sarana are busy living their lives, staring at their phones 24/7.

My friends at school are nice, but I can't relate to the things they're obsessed with; I feel like I don't belong there.

I feel like I don't belong anywhere.

I want to be with you.

There was silence for a beat, as the ocean of sleep rippled in soothing waves.

Then came the sound of a single caw, low-pitched and brief, just enough to interrupt his descent into sleep.

Neel found his eyes open, staring over the edge of the swing.

The fog must have cleared.

He could see the ground now.

And the ants.

They were spelling out a new message. The words rippled and changed as he read them, the same clusters of ants moving this way or that to reshape the words into new words, moving so fast that Neel had to read quickly to keep up.

OH DEAR BOY

I WISH YOU DID NOT HAVE TO GO THROUGH THIS

BUT

CHANGE IS A PART OF LIFE

BUT IT IS NOT ALL SAD

THERE IS JOY HAPPINESS FRIENDSHIP LOVE FAMILY

YOU MUST FIND THE JOY IN YOUR LIFE

FIND WHAT MAKES YOU HAPPY

WHAT LIGHTS YOU UP FROM WITHIN

GO TOWARDS THAT LIGHT

ENJOY IT

CELEBRATE IT

Out of the fog, from the direction of the roof, came a single sharp caw, like a warning.

'Neel!' Mama said, rushing toward him. 'Have you gone mad? You'll catch your death!'

Neel didn't argue as Mama led him inside, scolding him all the while, wrapping a warm quilt around him, a quilt embroidered by Nani with dancing elephants and playful, laughing Ganeshas. She forced him to drink hot milk with Bournvita as the rest of his family woke up to see what all the commotion was about.

Anmol and Sarana both teased him over breakfast about his new ambition to become a corpsicle.

Neel didn't complain or say anything.

He was still trying to process what the ants had spelled out.

* * *

Six weeks later, Neel sat on the swing again. The fog and cold had gone away. Warmer days were coming.

He couldn't see the ants, but he knew they were there.

He had talked to them many, many times over the past weeks.

Now, he spoke to them, not with his lips, but with his mind.

Nani, I was selected for the swim team today! Coach says I can be a good short sprint swimmer if I practise hard. I really like being in the water, using all my muscles. It feels like another world.

CONGRATS

EVEN WHEN YOU WERE A BABY YOU TRIED TO SWIM IN THE BATHTUB

I KNEW YOU WERE A BORN SWIMMER

I AM SO PROUD OF YOU

Without being aware that he was doing it, Neel said aloud, softly, 'Thank you, Nani! It's all thanks to you. And there's one more thing, Nani.'

YES

TELL ME

'Nani, I entered the art contest.'

ARRE WAH

JUST YESTERDAY YOU SAID YOU DID NOT WANT TO BE JUDGED

'I know,' he said, feeling a little ashamed, 'but I really want to show how well I can draw. Even my friends say I've gotten quite good. If I win the contest, then maybe Mama and Papa will agree to let me take the art course. Right now, they say it's too expensive for a hobby. Art is not just a hobby to me, Nani! It's my passion! I think when I go to college, I would like to study art and design. I want to be an artist.'

THAT SOUNDS WONDERFUL

DRAWING MAKES YOU HAPPY

'Very,' Neel said. 'When I'm drawing, I feel like I'm in another world within this world. My world. I can make of it whatever I want.'

YOUR DRAWINGS ARE BEAUTIFUL NEEL

I THINK YOU WILL BE A GREAT ARTIST SOMEDAY

'Aw, Nani,' he said, blushing, 'I'm just a learner!'

BUT TO ME YOU ARE MICHAELANGELO

'All I know,' Neel said seriously, 'is that it makes me happy. Very, very happy.'

YOU ARE FEELING BETTER NOW

NO MORE DARK THOUGHTS

'Papa and Mama also seem less worried. And even Anmol and Sarana have started treating me like a kid brother again. Not like a patient!'

SO HAPPY TO HEAR IT

DO WHAT MAKES YOU HAPPY

IF YOU ARE HAPPY YOU WILL MAKE PEOPLE AROUND YOU HAPPY TOO

AND THE WHOLE WORLD WILL BE A BETTER PLACE

NOW I HAVE TO TELL YOU SOMETHING

Neel had been lying on his stomach, looking down.

He sat up, holding on to the nylon ropes tightly.

Too tightly.

'What is it?' he asked, almost holding his breath.

I TOLD YOU WE WOULD ONLY BE ABLE TO TALK FOR SOME TIME

NOW THAT TIME HAS COME TO AN END

IT IS TIME FOR ME TO MOVE ON

AND FOR YOU TO MOVE ON TOO

Neel felt a moment of sadness come over him. But the shroud of darkness that had accompanied such feelings in the past wasn't there. He could see that the sadness would pass, that it was natural, and necessary, but it was not the whole world. There was more to life than just the sadness. So much more.

'I understand, Nani,' he said.

I HAVE ENJOYED EVERY MOMENT I SHARED WITH YOU NEEL

YOU ARE A VERY SPECIAL CHILD

AND YOU WILL GROW UP TO BE A VERY SPECIAL PERSON

I WILL ALWAYS LOVE YOU

AND WATCH OVER YOU

BUT FOR NOW IT IS TIME TO MOVE ON

I KNOW YOUR PAPA AND MAMA PLAN TO SELL THIS COTTAGE

I KNOW YOU WISH THEY WOULD NOT

BUT I AM FINE WITH IT

LET THEM SELL IT

THE MONEY WILL BE USEFUL

IT WILL HELP YOUR FAMILY

'Alright, Nani,' he murmured softly.

AND I WILL ALWAYS BE WITH YOU

IN YOUR HEART

YOUR MIND

YOUR SOUL

AND IN YOUR ART

GOODBYE NEEL

REMEMBER

YOU HAVE FOUND YOUR HAPPY PLACE

'Goodbye, Nani,' Neel said, 'I love you too.'

The ground rippled as the ants withdrew, disappearing to the far corners of the garden, to wherever it is that ants go when they are done with their chores, to their own happy place.

A gentle wind blew, caressing Neel's hair, tousling it, kissing his forehead. Summer was coming. The season of mangoes and holidays. He wiped the tears from his eyes.

Neel got down from the swing, looked around the garden one last time, then went inside the house. He had the sudden urge to draw.

On the rooftop of the old cottage, the lone crow sat perched for a while, looking this way then that.

Finally, he issued one final loud caw.

Then he flew away into the distance, cawing as he went.

Where Peacocks Dance

ADITHI RAO

Dadu's needle dives in and out of blue silk like fish playing in a pool of water. He creates patterns so beautiful that they make my breath catch. Dadu talks to himself as he stitches; his words are never audible. I try my best to understand, but in all my seven years I have never been able to make out a single word. Bits of dabka, those delicate, tightly coiled silver wires, slowly come together to make a pattern on the cloth. The only question is, what shape will they take today? A tree laden with fruit? A flower, maybe. A creeper, then? No wait, perhaps it will be a peacock!

Since I was a little girl, I have watched my grandfather turn pale lengths of cloth into magnificent dupattas, fit for brides and princesses! Everyone in Pandavpur knows that a wedding veil embroidered by Ali Razzaq Bhai will most certainly bring grace and good fortune upon the bride. Why only Pandavpur? People come from as far away as Lucknow and Delhi to have my grandfather embroider their wedding clothes with the zardozi kaarigari that he excels at.

As for me, I love to watch him work. I sit with my chin resting upon the edge of his wide, wooden work table, my eyes peeled to the needle as it slips through coils of wire and attaches them to the dupatta, which is held securely in place by a round wooden frame that ensures the stitches don't make the cloth bunch up and crumple.

I put out my hand to play with the dabka, so springy to the touch that they leap away and scatter on the floor. I scramble around to collect them, while Dadu smiles to himself and murmurs softly as he continues to embroider. Dadu never scolds or stops me from touching anything. Unless, of course, my hands are grubby.

One day I came to the workshop straight from petting Polki, the black-and-white spotted dog who lives in our street. When I eagerly caught up a piece of embroidery to examine my grandfather's fine handiwork more closely, my fingers left a grey smudge behind. That was the only time Dadu ever shook his head at me and tut-tutted.

'Always wash your hands before you touch the cloth, bitiya,' he said, adding gently, '*Yeh kisi ki amaanat hai, na?*' What that means, in case you don't understand Urdu, is that the cloth had been handed over to him in trust.

Abashed by his mild reprimand, I ran away to wash. It was a little late for that, I agree, but who knew when next my fingers might reach out without my consent and touch something else? Since that day I have always taken care to clean my hands before entering the workshop. You know, I plan to be a kaarigar like him someday.

'Na-na,' Dadu says, when I share my ambition with him while we walk through the mustard fields on the edge of Pandavpur. (We are trying to catch the setting sun before it escapes over the horizon.) 'Not kaarigari. You must study hard and find something good to do with your life. Become a teacher. Or a doctor maybe. Something that will make you very happy.'

'But zardozi makes me happy, Dadu. Besides, if I do any other work then I will have to go out every morning, instead of sitting here stitching by your side.'

I look up at him expectantly, and he chuckles in reply. When I turn, it is to see that the wily sun has slipped away from under my nose again! It has left behind for me a blaze of golden pink and orange light in a once-blue sky.

* * *

Today Ammi has told me to come straight home from school because I have to study for my maths test. I hate maths, so of course Ammi always makes me study it. Bah!

'Let the little one come to the workshop as usual,' Dadu suggests. 'I'll teach her.'

Ammi looks relieved, but I frown. What does Dadu know about subtraction? He never went to school, never attended the second grade like

I do now. Khair, I may as well go. Anything is better than sitting at home doing sums under Ammi's stern eye. Besides, maybe I will be able to distract Dadu into taking me to the market to buy ice candies, and we'll end up studying nothing at all! Pleased with my plan, I dash out of the school grounds the moment Ramu Chacha rings the going-home bell and head straight for the workshop. As I kick off my slippers at the entrance, I hear Dadu talking to someone. His words are clear now. There must be someone in there with him. A visitor, maybe.

'...you *are* free,' he insists. 'Don't you want to dance?'

His voice trails away, his tone affectionate like when he is trying to convince me to drink my milk (which I hate). I feel a dart of jealousy and hurry inside to glance around quickly. There is nobody in the room. My scowl fades.

'Who were you talking to?' I demand curiously.

'Never you mind, little monkey,' he replies with a naughty smile. I toss my school bag aside thinking to myself: *He is getting old. That's why he talks to himself so much.* I squat down beside him, curious to see the progress he has made since I left for school this morning. But Dadu will have none of that today.

'Put your bag away neatly in that corner and take out your copy book, bitiya,' he says. 'Now come here and look at this.' He spreads a length of red satin on the table and lays a measuring tape across it. '98 centimetres. Write that number down.'

Ya Allah! What does subtraction have to do with cloth? Dadu jerks his head insistently towards my notebook, and reluctantly I write down the measurement.

'Now,' Dadu continues, 'if I cut out a length from one corner to make a sleeve...here, see, this much. Now how much will be left over for the rest of the blouse?'

'Dadu?'

'Hmm?'

'Does the bride have only one arm?'

Dadu frowns in puzzlement. '*Nahin, kyun?*'

'Then why does the wedding blouse have only one sleeve?'

I fall back in a fit of giggles, tickled by my own wit. Dadu joins in with deep guffaws. When the moment passes, he pats me on the back and says, 'Maths is important to a tailor.' This makes me prick up my ears. No matter what Dadu said the other day in the mustard field, I haven't changed my mind about becoming a kaarigar. We return to the lesson, and I listen carefully this time. And that is how I come to learn subtraction from a measuring tape and a piece of cloth.

Quite proud of my little foray into the mysteries of mathematics, I race Polki back home. It is night now, and dinner is over. I search my school bag for my maths notebook, emptying its contents higgledy-piggledy onto the floor. The book is nowhere to be found. Did Polki eat it? No, she was too busy racing me home to have done so. Did it fall out of my bag when I ran? Unlikely. The flap of the bag had been closed tightly. Then where could my notebook be?

In a flash I remember seeing it lying on Dadu's worktable back in the shop. I don't remember putting it back in my bag though, so it must still be there. I have to retrieve it, there are three unfinished sums to complete and turn in to Asha Miss in the morning.

I cross over to Dadu's room, where I find him fast asleep with his glasses on his nose, snoring so loudly that his white moustache stands up in the air with every breath, looking very funny! I giggle. Poor Dadu, how to wake him up? He's so tired, let him sleep. Maybe I can slip out of the house and go fetch my book before Ammi realizes I've gone. It is just two lanes away; with any luck she may not even notice my absence. Good idea! I fish out the workshop keys from the pocket of Dadu's shirt hanging on the hook by the door, making sure that they don't jangle. Clutching them firmly in my hand, I tiptoe to the door, but return to Dadu's side to carefully ease the glasses off his face. For a moment I gaze down at him, the deep grooves around his mouth, the thin cheeks, the wrinkles. There are lines at the corners of his eyes, put there by laughter and kindness. I smile to myself and slip away by the back entrance.

Minutes later, I turn on the switch inside the workshop. The naked bulb overhead springs to life, lighting up the room and leaving only the corners in shadows. I have never been here at this hour. Everything seems so strange and unfamiliar somehow. As if something is different. Something is...*missing*. But what? I peer at the box of needles and the rows of colourful silk threads neatly wound around reels. The finished dupattas, those that are ready to be delivered to their owners hang neatly from wooden hangers by the... Wait a minute. Only the finished pieces are usually put on hangers. Yet the ones here are just lengths of bare satin and silk. Where are the peacocks, then? Where are the creepers and flowers and fruit trees that Dadu has spent months creating with his needle?

Somebody has stolen the embroidery from the dupattas, my brain screams! I spin on my heel and charge outside, forgetting, in my hurry, to lock the doors of the workshop behind me. Back in the house, Ammi is still humming to herself as she washes the utensils.

I run straight to Dadu and shake him awake. He sits bolt upright and looks at me, startled. I put a finger to my lips and tug on his arm. Sensing my urgency, he follows me out of the house without a word. We step into the workshop together and I point to the empty panels of cloth, aghast. To my utter bewilderment, Dadu throws back his head and laughs! Now I'm convinced that my grandfather has taken leave of his senses.

The shock must be too much for him, I think. *First thing in the morning Abbu and I will take him to Dr Katiyar. I'll tell Doctor Chacha about all the weird stuff that's been going on with Dadu. The talking to himself, the bouts of random laughter. Maybe an injection will help. But what if Dadu has to have an operation to set him right?*

My heart goes cold at the thought. An injection is bad enough...

'Come, bitiya,' Dadu says. He leads me away from the workshop and in the direction of the mustard fields. I follow, heart thumping in my chest. When we reach the fields, the light from the full moon has turned the whole world silver.

I glance at Dadu, but he keeps on walking. There is an air of secrecy about him, a sense of mystery all around. When he slows down, I do too. He smiles and puts a finger to his lips. This world is familiar, and yet I feel like I have never been here before. Dadu pulls me behind a nearby tree and points to something in the distance. A peacock! A peacock that has shaken out its splendid feathers and is dancing among the flowers! The blue-green wings, the turn of its head, where have I seen these before? Why, it is Dadu's peacock, the same one he embroidered two days ago! And it is not alone. There are others there, dancing with it. The dabkas and crystals sewed into their tails catch the moonlight, making my heart soar. The roses that Dadu embroidered last month, the little birds and dainty gazelles, the creepers from Sharmila didi's wedding dupatta are all here in this field, dancing under the moonlit sky...

'Dadu,' I whisper, 'It was them you were speaking to all along, wasn't it? *You* sent them here to play!' I read the answer in his old-old eyes that glow with mirth and magic.

Something hard lands on the top of my head. 'Uff!' I look up, startled, rubbing my pate. A pear has dropped out of the tree under which we stand. It is laden with fruit, this tree that was never here before tonight. I pick up the fallen pear and bite into it.

'Shukriya,' I whisper to its branches...

Hide and Seek

VARSHA SESHAN

The four cousins hopped from foot to foot. They wrung their hands. They licked their lips. They switched on their best puppy eyes.

'Plee-e-e-e-ase!' begged Mahesh. 'A teeny-tiny nibble. A lick. A—'

Paati's eyes glinted behind her spectacles. 'No.'

Puppy faces worked when the cousins wanted ice cream.

Big, round, innocent eyes worked when they wanted to play a little longer.

Cajoling and cuddling worked when they wanted money to buy sweet bread from across the road.

But nothing worked when it came to this one thing—munching Diwali treats before Diwali. Paati was immune to it all.

It was Diya's turn. 'Please, Paati, please. Just... just one muthusaram. We'll share it. All four of us will share it.' If that wasn't a noble offer, she didn't know what was.

Mahesh wrinkled his nose at her. One muthusaram amongst them was nothing. But in Diya's defence, he had also come down to begging for just a lick.

Paati chuckled. She enjoyed the annual conversation. And she'd been having it for much longer—first with her own children, now with her grandchildren. 'No. On Diwali and after Diwali, you can eat as many muthusarams as you want.'

Samit clasped his hands. 'What about a laddu? Just one laddu?'

'We could just taste them and tell you if they're okay,' said Jyoti. 'We'll be the testing, tasting squad. TTS. Like, like a...'

'Quality check,' supplied Diya. 'We'll do a quality check.' She looked at Paati and added, as an afterthought, 'Please?'

Paati's eyes twinkled. 'I've been making the same things every year for forty years. If you still think a quality check is required, maybe I should retire and—'

'No, no, no!' protested the cousins together. Store-bought Diwali snacks were never the same. Paati had to make them. That was the fun of Diwali.

'What about—' began Mahesh.

'What about...?' prompted Paati.

'Nothing,' said Mahesh with an angelic smile.

Paati wagged her finger. 'What mischief are you planning?'

'Nothing!' repeated Mahesh. He skipped out of the room. 'Nothing, nothing, *no*thing!'

The cousins never stopped trying. That was part of the fun of Diwali—trying to persuade Paati to let them taste everything she made. Of course, it was for all of them anyway. The rule, however, was that they could eat it only on and after Diwali.

But when the smells of cooking were in the air, when their mouths watered—and most importantly, when they were not allowed to eat the snacks—that's when it was most fun.

The cousins trooped into the room where all four of them slept.

'What was that about?' asked Jyoti.

Mahesh's eyes sparkled. 'I was going to say—what if we find Paati's hiding place? Could we taste the muthusaram then?'

'Why didn't you ask, then?' asked Diya.

'Duh! Because obviously then Paati would say "no"! This way...'

Putting on their best innocent faces yet again, they began to search. They searched the kitchen and Paati's room thoroughly, only when she was not looking of course. How could Paati hide huge steel boxes? Who could hide huge steel boxes anywhere, except maybe if you buried them underground?

And it wasn't just one set of snacks. The smells they'd woken up to over the last week were proof that she had made two sweets—jangiri and laddu—and two savouries—muthusaram and omapodi—as usual. It was just a matter of finding them.

They split up and began to hunt.

They searched the lofts and the cupboards, even Paati's cupboard, which smelled of silk and camphor.

Jyoti pushed open the creaky bathroom door and scanned the bathroom cabinets.

'How would she hide them there?' scoffed Samit. 'The cabinets are tiny, and—'

'No harm looking,' said Jyoti, and marched off to look in the trunk in the balcony.

'Hunt in the most obvious places too,' hissed Diya. 'Like in the steel boxes in plain sight. Some may be full!'

'Be careful,' warned Jyoti. 'If Paati catches us hunting...'

Paati chuckled behind them, and the cousins jumped. 'Don't you know that I've successfully hidden everything for years? If your fathers didn't find them...'

'Hmph.' Diya scowled. They had to search even harder.

The steel boxes in plain sight were, of course, empty. It was time to search deep inside the house.

'I know!' whispered Diya. 'She may have given the boxes to Sejal Aunty!'

Sure that they'd hit upon the secret, the cousins did a little victory dance before sneaking out.

And found the house locked.

'Sejal goes to Matheran for Diwali every year,' said Paati from the doorway. The cousins jumped again. Paati would have made an excellent spy. 'She can't stand the noise of the city.' She smiled innocently, as innocently as her grandchildren, and asked, 'Did you want something from her?'

Hours later, Diya slumped on the sofa. 'I give up,' she declared, folding her arms across her chest.

Paati smiled. 'What about you?' she asked the others.

Mahesh made a face and switched on the TV.

Jyoti gave their grandmother a weak smile.

'Someday,' said Samit, darkly. 'Someday, we'll find it.'

Paati grinned. 'Diwali will come before your *someday*!'

Diya grumped. Unfortunately, that seemed more than a little likely.

Besides, there were a hundred other fun things to do—shopping, rangoli, painting diyas, packing dry fruits to distribute to neighbours and friends... Every so often, one of them would think of a new place and excitedly fling open a cupboard to check, only to have their hopes dashed once more.

The day before Diwali, all the work was done.

Brand-new clothes hung in the cupboard, ready to be worn predawn the next day.

The dry fruits had been distributed and there were extra packets in the kitchen cupboard, in case unexpected guests came over.

All the diyas were painted and filled with oil, ready to line the terrace parapet once the sun set.

'Shall we play hide and seek?' suggested Samit.

'Yes!'

Mahesh began to count, and the others fled.

Diya's eyes darted everywhere.

From the next room, Mahesh's voice rang out, '45-46-47-48-49…'

'Aaah! Where-to-hide-where-to-hide-where…' Diya scurried about like a headless chicken. 'Paati! Please, I want to—' She stopped. Mahesh was counting far too fast for her to waste time. She went down on her knees and crawled behind her grandmother's legs and under the huge divan.

'Diya, the—' Paati broke off. She was too good a sport to give Diya's hiding place away.

Under the divan, Diya put her hand over her mouth to hold back her giggle. Paati's sari was perfect. Diya could stay perfectly hidden under there.

The problem, though, was that there used to be lizards—and maybe even mice—under the ancient divan. Paati always said it was too heavy to move and clean properly. Diya pulled her legs into her chest, looking around warily. Surely, there were no lizards now. Did lizards even like the floor?

'Samit, you're out!' cried Mahesh.

Diya heard Samit grumbling as he came out from behind the curtain. Diya bit back her smile. Samit always chose the easiest hiding places.

Cautiously, Diya peeped out from behind Paati's sari. She could see Mahesh's feet tiptoeing around the living room. The red and blue divan cover did not reach all the way to the floor. Diya bit her lip and drew back closer, to the wall. Even if there were no lizards, there would be dirt. Dirt that was months old, if not years old. If she put grubby hands on the fresh cover, Paati would—

Diya nearly cried out, as she jerked her hand away. There was something under the divan! In the little light that filtered into the room, she could not make out what it was. Tentatively, she reached out again.

Steel.

Steel boxes.

A smile crept onto Diya's face. That's where the muthusarams and jangiris and laddus were! The lizard and rat stories were just ways to keep children away! Biting her lip, she began to prise open the jar. She would emerge with the best prize of all. She would...

Diya stopped.

Paati had not given Diya's hiding place away.

'No one's around,' whispered Paati.

'I found them!' Diya whispered back.

'And? Are you going to sit there and eat them?'

A long, long pause followed.

'No.' Diya's voice sounded grumpy even to her own ears. Voices argued inside her head, but she sighed. If Paati could be nice enough... She shook her head.

Mahesh strode back into the room, accompanied this time by Samit and Jyoti. Deliberately, Diya shook the bed cover slightly.

'I spy Diya!' cried Mahesh, jumping up and down. 'Caught you! Caught you! Nya-nya-nya-nya-nya!'

Diya crawled out from under the divan. Not surprisingly, her clothes were perfectly clean, without even a speck of dust on them.

'Thank you, Paati, for not giving away my hiding place,' she said, pointedly.

With Mahesh celebrating his victory loud enough to drown everything else out, Paati muttered back, 'Thank you, Diya, for not giving away my hiding place.'

Diya grinned. In a few hours, it would be Diwali.

My Grandmother and Her Daughter

HARSHIKAA UDASI

'Ammi, Ammiiii!'

'What? What happened?' my grandmother exclaimed, startled, as she reached for her glasses.

'Ammi, it's time for tea, that's all,' I smiled at her. 'You fell asleep on the rocking chair. As usual.'

'No, no. I never fall asleep. You just feel like I am sleeping. I'm actually meditating, you silly girl,' said my grandmother, straightening herself.

'Aha! Just meditating? Papa came, touched your feet, got that tap fixed with Ashraf chacha's help, told you bye and went, and you didn't move a bit. And, of course, you were just meditating!' I exclaimed.

Ammi laughed. She never got mad at me. Even if I teased her all day long. I was too much like her Nandu. Everyone knew that my eyes reminded her of her daughter. Big, bright, and forever questioning. When Nandu bua was ten, Ammi would often tell her not to knit her eyebrows into a question all the time. 'You look so funny, Nandu. Your face will get stuck like that. Then no one will marry you,' she would tell her. 'Very good then, I will always keep my eyebrows like that. Then no one will marry me! What can be better than that?' Nandu would retort.

Nandu bua would have been fifty-six now. If only her little hand hadn't slipped out of Ammi's that night in August 1947. If only Ammi had managed to spot her in the sea of people thronging Karachi port. If only someone would have somehow miraculously returned their tiny ten-year-old to my grandparents. If only they wouldn't have had to leave their home. If only there had been no Partition. If only...

My grandmother was lost in her thoughts again, just as I was.

'Meditating again?' I asked, handing her her much-loved evening chai. Ma was not at home, and I had somehow managed to make tea. It was nothing like the chai Ammi loved. She smiled at the first sip. 'Wah! Garam sherbet. Indira Chandan, when I was your age, I could manage an entire household of fifteen people, help my mother-in-law cook four times a day and handle a battery of manservants—the strong, tall Pathans. At least chai you must make properly!'

'Madam Ishwari Chandan, that was 1940. In the 1990s, I have more things to do than make chai!' I retorted, but seeing the look in her eyes, I mellowed down.

Ammi laughed. She always did when I called her Madam Ishwari Chandan. But now I wasn't sure if she was laughing at that or my tea.

'Like what, knit? You can't hold the needles together! Stitch? You can't even thread the needle! Cook? Can't roll out...' Ammi started counting my abilities on her fingers.

'Okay, okay. But I can sing, and I can write, and I am the topper of my class. Doesn't that matter?'

'My child, that's all that does. Nothing else matters,' said Ammi, pulling me by the ear and kissing me on my forehead. 'Okay, tell me one thing. Why do you not call me Dadi?'

Resting my chin on the arm of the unsteady rocking chair, I smiled. 'Because Papa and Ma call you that and so did Nandu bua, Papa tells me. Back in Sindh, everybody called their mother Ammi, right? I just love the sound of it.'

Ammi shut her eyes. I knew I had touched a raw nerve.

'You still remember every little thing about her, no?' I gently asked my grandmother.

She looked at me for a long time. 'I am never alone, Indu. Nandu's voice is with me all the time. How can I ever forgive myself for losing my little daughter as we fled what was, almost overnight, declared Pakistan? I could never forgive your Nana for not looking for her and making us board that ship instead. All of us had left behind our life's earnings, our home, and some unfortunate ones, like Gobind and me, even a part of our family that we would never see again.'

'I understand, Ammi, but forty-six years is a long time. Isn't it long enough to forgive and long enough to forget?' I said softly. My parents had reasoned with her several times, but Ammi would still get deeply disturbed when the scene flashed before her eyes.

'Easy for you to say that. But those who had left everything and everyone behind in Sindh during the Partition could never really forgive or forget. Maybe your generation will be the last to even know about the divide, the separation, the loss, and the pain. Maybe nobody cares any longer,' she said, keeping aside her teacup. She sighed. 'Even Gobind didn't care. How could he not have grieved? How could he have erased Nandu so conveniently from his memory? He only spoke about how people haggled for a packet of papad, how he couldn't source jars for the pickle that day, or how he might have to sell off my last gold bangle the next day. Just nothing at all about Nandu. Just nothing at all about Sindh.'

But I knew that my grandfather had cared. About a lot of things. He had brought his wife and their son at 1 a.m. into the last ship leaving Karachi for Bombay. If you missed it, you would certainly be killed. If you got on to it, you left behind everything. Gobindram Chandan, who was exhausted, bewildered, and frightened, wasn't sure about his choice. In his pocket were 500 rupees, and on one arm lay his wife Ishwari, partly conscious. That night of August 20, 1947, had changed it all. Till yesterday, he was Lala Gobindram, owner of the famous Chaman Dryfruits. Today he was fleeing his homeland. By tomorrow, he would be a refugee. Minutes ago, he was the father of two. Now he comforted his hungry son with some limp biscuits as he wondered if they would ever see their daughter Nandu again.

My Ammi had never understood his side of the story. She was still hurting. She hadn't slept a single night in the last forty-six years. As she lay on her bed, she clutched at her bedsheet as though it were her daughter's hand. She hadn't wept for anything after that night. Not when they had had to eat stale pav and dal at the refugee camp, not even when my grandfather had had to go door-to-door selling papads and pickles which she prepared to earn a living. People were surprised when she did not even shed a tear at his death.

The clock chiming six brought us out of our stupor.

'I will just walk down to the temple, Indu,' Ammi said, wiping her mouth with the pallu of her white saree and looking around for her slippers. 'Do you want to come too? Vineeta will also be there.'

Talking to Vineeta aunty would make her feel better and the temple was close by. Going alone wouldn't be such a problem, would it? 'I have a lot to study this evening. In fact, Papa also asked Ma to return quickly from the shop. He is going to be back in half an hour as well. He had suggested you drop the temple idea and pray at home, Ammi. The time is such.'

'You know I always go to the temple on eighth January. I will go and come back soon. And you don't need to worry. This is our own area. Hindus and Muslims have always lived together here. We are not crazy like the fools outside. It is past six o'clock and the aarti will begin shortly. I will be back in an hour, okay?'

Of course. It was Nandu bua's birthday. I also knew that it was 1993 in Mumbai.

As Ammi walked out of our flat on the ground floor of our chawl, Mumbai was simmering. Riots between Hindus and Muslims had broken out. Ishwari Chandan had seen it forty-six years ago when the country had been divided—communities that lived in complete harmony picking up swords. It was not a fire that would die down quickly.

None of us knew that the next hour of her life would turn our lives around.

* * *

Ishwari Chandan was shuffling along the street, when she saw their plumber, Ashraf chacha, smiling cautiously at her. 'How are you, Ashraf bhaijaan?' she asked. 'I am fine, Aapa. But what are you doing here now?' he responded, looking slightly worried.

'Why? This is our own locality, right? Or are you also worried about our safety now? What is this, Ashraf bhaijaan? What will anyone do to a seventy-one-year-old?' she laughed.

'No Aapa, please go home. The time is not right,' he said, looking around, the worry now very real.

'What's happened to you? Are you...' Ishwari's question was halted midway as she heard a loud cry from one end of the street. She stood rooted to the ground. Mobs horrified her, and this was one of the largest she had seen. As large as the one she was caught in so many years ago. She zipped around looking for Ashraf, but he ran away while shouting out names. 'Salim! Asgar! Ready?' One elderly lady shoved her into a corner. 'Want to die or what? Go home,' she screeched into her ear. Ishwari crouched behind a wall. Her home was just five buildings away, but she couldn't go across in the hail of shattering glass and flying brickbats.

'Don't people have to go to work? Don't they have to send their children to school? Doesn't everyone want a safe and secure life without having to worry about violence?' Ishwari thought as her eyes darted from one vengeful face to the other. They seemed like hardened criminals, all of them. But soon, she could recognize several known faces among them. Firoz was in a group of four destroying Meena's small flower shop. Wasn't that the milkman's son, Ritesh, who had a flaming torch in his hand?

'Ammi,' she heard a feeble voice. 'Ammmiiii!' A small hand clasped her wrinkled fingers. 'Huh? Who are you?' asked Ishwari, trying to recognize the face of the little girl with messy hair and a sweaty face looking up at her. 'Please take me to my Ammi.' The girl was about ten. 'What's your name? Where do you stay?' asked Ishwari in hushed tones. 'Saira...Saira...next lane. Please take me to my Ammi. These people will not let me go,' she pleaded.

Nandu must have pleaded like this. Who would have heard her? Was she in Pakistan? Or did someone push her into the ship knowing that many Hindus were on it and she was just an innocent girl separated from her family? Or was she...?

'Ammi, will you take me home? Please?' cried the young girl. Those eyes. How could anyone say no? Ishwari was unsure if her legs had the strength, but she began thinking of ways to get to the girl's home. 'Ammi, I know how to get home, but I don't want to go alone there. Will you be able to walk?' said the girl, suddenly realizing that Ishwari was very old. 'You don't worry. Hold my hand. And remember, don't ever leave it. Okay?' Could she take this child to safety, unlike the one she had lost in 1947?

The duo made their way over the debris from the rioting and crossed a low wall separating the two colonies. Their fingers were tightly wound around each other's. Neither could let go. Neither wanted to let go.

'Hey, who is that?' a brusque voice made them stop in their tracks. Ishwari and Saira turned to see an unknown man brandishing a large knife in his hand. Was he Hindu, or was he Muslim? Who must they say they were? And would he believe them? Ishwari's thoughts were flying, trying to gauge what would happen next. 'You are Dinesh chacha's mother, right? Why are you out at this time, aunty?' he softened his tone. Then he cast a glance at the girl holding her hand. 'Who is she? She is not ours, is she?'

Ishwari wondered, what did it mean—not 'ours'? Who is 'ours' and who is not? The man asked again, 'Aunty, who is she? Where are you from, girl?' His voice became gruff again, even as he threatened to come closer. 'Beta, this is my friend's granddaughter. She wanted to go to the temple, so I got her along,' Ishwari blurted the first thing that passed through her numb brain. The man glared at Saira, but then turned away. 'Okay, aunty, but this is no time to go to the temple. Go home,' he shouted as he walked away.

In the next five minutes, they went past shuttered shops and locked homes, ducking flying stones, holding on to each other till they reached a shack with a tin sheet for a door. With her free hand, Saira banged vigorously and shouted, 'Abbuuuu, Ammiiiiii!' The tin door immediately opened, and the worried parents rushed forward and hugged their little one. 'Saira, where were you? Abbu just came in after looking for you!' cried her mother, tears streaming down her face. Ishwari looked on, not realizing that Saira's hand was still firmly clenched in her own.

'Those parents could have been us,' she thought. 'All those years ago, someone could have returned my Nandu to Gobind and me that fateful night.'

'Ammi, thank you!' Saira turned to her and gave her a smile that filled Ishwari's heart with warmth. She caressed the young girl's face for a long moment, looking into her eyes as though searching for something. Then, called back into the present by the noises around them, she asked the child to go into the safety of her home. 'Go, Nandu. Now you are safe,' Ishwari said softly.

'You can leave my hand now, Ammi! And my name is Saira, not Nandu!' Those eyes danced even after going through so much in the last half an hour.

This time, Ishwari hadn't yet let go of the little fingers. She slowly opened her fingers finally releasing the child's hand. This time there was no fear, no anxiety. Saira was home. Nandu was fine. 'Aapa, please come inside and sit in our home till this reckless storm passes. It is small, but you will be safe here,' said Saira's father. 'No, bhaijaan. My family is waiting, and I believe there is still some goodness left in this world. It should see me through to my home,' said Ishwari.

'Ammi!' called out Saira as Ishwari made to walk back, 'Go carefully!' Ishwari smiled at her.

Twenty minutes later, Ashraf bhaijaan escorted Ishwari safely back home. 'Aapa, I told you to return then itself. Why did you have to take this risk? So much danger outside!' he said, admonishing her.

'What to do, bhaijaan? I had to take someone to safety. See, as you did for me,' she smiled.

* * *

That evening as I opened the door, my Ammi looked different. Her wrinkled eyes seemed to be at peace. 'Ammi is back!' I cried, calling out to my parents but she, I clearly remember, had a soft smile on her lips.

The next day's newspapers were full of terrible news about Mumbai. For some people, however, it was a different story altogether. After forty-six long years, Ammi finally slept well at night.

My Ammi had saved her Nandu.

The Forbidden Room

ANDALEEB WAJID

Summer vacations were here and Maya was excited about visiting her grandparents. They lived in a tiny village and it often felt like she was in a museum when she was there. Everything was just so very old!

The furniture looked like it had been made in the early 1900s and maybe it had been. Her grandparents lived in a huge mansion-like house on the outskirts of the village. There were lots of trees there and usually she and her brother Rohit would challenge each other to see who could climb the highest.

Even though he was two years younger, he was nimbler for some reason and could climb trees like a monkey. Every summer vacation, both of them would stay out in the sun, turning brown while Amma yelled at them, reminding them to use sunscreen.

'Sunscreen is for girls!' Rohit yelled back.

'No, it's not just for girls. It's for everyone,' Maya reprimanded him but they were both reluctant to get down from the trees and head back inside right away. So much of their life in Bangalore was spent indoors that they just didn't want to stay within four walls when there was so much freedom to explore here.

On some days, she and Rohit would skip to the nearby stream and dangle their feet in the cold, sludgy water and lie back on the ground, staring up at the sky as the clouds scudded past them.

But once it was evening, they had to both return, wash up outside in the courtyard and go inside where Ajji would be waiting for them with badam milk and lots of crunchy snacks.

All of life should be a summer vacation, Maya thought dreamily. But summer vacations can also get disrupted. That year, a sudden rainstorm kept them inside the house for days on end. Both Rohit and Maya were bored out of their minds. The Internet was spotty and there was no Wi-Fi either.

When the rain didn't seem like it would let up, Maya decided she was going to check out that room upstairs where no one ever went. Every year she visited her grandparents, she wanted to explore that room but it was always locked and her mother told her no one knew what was inside. There was a huge padlock on the door and it felt mysterious and a bit forbidding.

She was also a little scared of her grandfather who was tall, had a bristling moustache and walked everywhere with his back erect and his cane tapping the ground thunderously. Maya and Rohit stayed out of his way as best as they could. Ma, too, avoided being around her father. Maya wondered if Ajja had been this way as a baby too. When she asked Ajji, her grandmother burst out laughing.

'How would I know how he was as a baby?' she asked, rocking back and forth on the wooden pallet she was sitting as she strung jasmine buds into a garland. 'I wasn't even born when he was a baby.'

'There must have been photos or something?' Maya persisted.

At that, Ajji looked up in the direction of that forbidden room and Maya's pulse quickened. Something was there, definitely. But Ajji immediately changed the subject.

'Here, find that next episode of that serial and give it to me?' she asked, putting away the jasmine buds and handing her phone to Maya.

Maya was exasperated. Ajji had learnt how to use her smartphone but whenever she went to YouTube she got distracted by the ads and clicked on everything that she saw, with the result being that she would watch something absurd about how some famous actor had died but everyone had kept it a huge secret from the world.

'Ajji, just type the name of the serial and the episode number here, in the search bar,' Maya explained to her.

Ajji squinted at the screen and sighed. 'I know, I know. I try but sometimes I find something so interesting completely by chance. Did you know that there is a town in some mountain place where all the cats have three legs?'

'Ayyo, Ajji. Don't fall for all that stuff!' Maya said. She entered the name of the TV show and handed it to Ajji.

'Fine, fine,' Ajji muttered as she took it from her.

The rain pounded in earnest outside, and Maya sighed. Rohit was sketching something on his notepad but she was really bored.

'Can I go up to that room and see what's inside?' she asked Ajji, hoping to get her permission when she was distracted. To her dismay, Ajji put down the phone.

'Your Ajja has forbidden anyone to enter that room,' she said quietly. 'No one is allowed to go in.'

But Maya was tired of listening to everyone and being a good girl. She had seen where Ajja kept the key to the huge padlock that was used to lock the room. She knew that he slept in the afternoons, sitting on his reclining wooden chair and she also knew that most of the household took their afternoon naps at the same time. So she decided she would get hold of the key and go inside and take a look.

That afternoon, she waited until everyone had retired for their nap and she walked up to where Ajja was sleeping. She felt a little nervous as she quietly peeked under the chair and spotted the small tin box where he kept the key. She pulled it out slowly, all the time looking at him to see whether he had awakened. Her heart raced and she was scared that she would get caught. But Ajja continued to sleep, snoring softly.

She turned back and saw that Ajji was asleep on the diwan too. Rohit and Amma were in the room where they slept at nights, also taking a nap. Amma had asked her to join them for an afternoon nap but Maya had escaped, making up some excuse.

In minutes, she was outside the room, inserting the key into the rusty padlock, her hands trembling as she wondered what she might encounter inside. What was the big secret? Why didn't anyone *ever* go inside? The door opened creakily and Maya expelled her breath, realizing she had been holding it for so long.

A cobweb dangled in front of her like it did in horror films and she brushed it away impatiently but also wary, in case there were spiders with the cobweb. The room was dark and musty except for a little light that came in from a window right at the top. Dust motes danced in the meagre light and she wondered if there was a light switch anywhere.

The sound of the rain seemed magnified here for some reason and that sent a shiver of fear down her spine. After running her palms across the grimy wall, she found a wooden switch box with a circular plastic switch that was common in this house. She pulled down the switch and a yellow bulb flickered to life directly under the ceiling.

She quickly scanned the room, and saw that there was a heavy-looking tin chest in one corner. The rest of the room was empty except for some rags on the floor, a few broken chairs and some dirty woven mats.

This was disappointing to say the least. She had been expecting to find something interesting, something that would help her while away the afternoon without getting bored.

She knelt before the chest and tried to lift up the lid. It was heavy but she managed to open it. Her disappointment grew when she saw that there was nothing very exciting inside. Just some old mouldy books, bound with deep green cardboard.

Feeling annoyed and irritated, she picked up one and opened it. Her eyes widened when she saw what they were.

Comics! She checked the other books also quickly. All of them were comics! Maya loved comics although her mother detested them. Amma thought that children shouldn't read comics because they were not good for broadening their minds and it didn't count as reading. Even so, Maya had a stack back at home, a huge collection of DC and Marvel comics.

Amma groaned whenever she saw her with the comics, lamenting that they were of no use at all.

'Read something that will teach you new words. That will help you write better essays in school!'

Maya knew that telling her she found such books boring would result in a comic ban, so she often nodded and pretended to read something her mother thrust at her.

Which comics were these, she wondered. She sat down on the floor and opened one of the bound books.

Phantom.

She flipped open another one.

Mandrake the Magician.

I've *never* heard of this guy, she thought as she crossed her legs and started reading.

She didn't know how long she had been sitting there, absorbed in the wonderful world of the Ghost Who Walks and the amazing adventures of Mandrake and his friends. The comics had yellowed pages and the sharp smell made her sneeze a couple of times. But she persisted. These were fun!

It felt like they were from another lifetime altogether. The clothes, the way the people talked, the cars, the fights with the kaboom and the kapow written as if the words were indeed punching their way out of the pages!

Ajja's cane thumped on the floor. She jumped, shocked that she had been so lost in reading, she hadn't noticed when he'd come upstairs. She looked behind her to see him looking at her grimly.

'Why did you come here?' he asked softly. She quickly scrambled up, one of the comic books still in her hand.

'I...I just wanted to know what was here!' she stammered. When Ajja didn't reply, she mustered enough courage to ask him, 'Why are all these comics here?'

To her surprise, a pained expression flitted across his face. 'My father,' he said, simply. He moved forward slowly and Maya was glad to see that he wasn't angry. He looked tired and old. She no longer felt scared of him.

'I used to love reading these comics when I was your age,' he continued as he leaned into the chest. 'Aah...*Phantom* was my favourite,' he said, picking up one book gingerly and batting it gently to dislodge the dust.

'I used to collect these books and come up here to read them. This was my room, you know,' he said, looking around.

Maya let him speak, listening to a different time of life altogether. She'd wanted to know what Ajja was like as a child. Well, he was telling her himself!

'My father hated these comics. He said that they interfered in my studies and one year when I performed badly in school, he said I couldn't buy or read anymore. He made me promise that I wouldn't come up here again to read them.'

'That's *just* like Amma!' Maya said, surprised. 'She too hates comics! Did you do the same to her?'

Ajja shook his head, a wry smile on his face. 'I didn't need to. She wasn't interested in reading at all. But I see that you have inherited my love for comics.'

Maya looked down at the book in her hand and said, 'Yes. I do read other books as well, but I love comics too. Amma says they're a waste of time and they don't do anything to improve my knowledge.'

Ajja's face was wreathed in a wider smile. 'She must have got that from my father. And you apparently are like me!'

Maya stared at him in surprise. When Ajja smiled, he didn't look so scary at all.

'It's been twenty years since my father died. I think some promises can be broken after such a long period. Don't you think?' he asked.

Maya nodded.

'Come.' Ajja said, taking her hand. 'We'll get this room cleaned up and you and I can sit together and enjoy reading the comics.'

'And what about Amma?' she asked, delighted but also nervous.

'Your mother knows better than to interfere with my plans,' Ajja replied, this time with a twinkle in his eye.

Viva Magenta

MENAKA RAMAN

Nandu woke up with a start, with a weird sensation running down the back of her neck—the kind you get when you feel like you're not alone. She reached out and switched on her night lamp before slipping her glasses on, sighing with relief as the room came into focus.

At the edge of her bed sat her grandmother.

'Well?' Paati asked expectantly.

'Well what?' asked Nandu sleepily.

'What do you think?' Paati smiled.

'What do I think?' repeated Nandu.

'Okay, let's stop. We could be doing this all night,' huffed her grandmother. 'What do you think of my hair?'

It was then that Nandu's eyes snagged onto her grandmother's thick white hair that was always tamed into a no-nonsense bun. Now, in place of the bun, was a super short, super stylish bob.

'You cut your hair!' Nandu gasped.

'I did! I cut it all off. It feels like this huge weight has been lifted off...well my head, not my shoulders,' smiled Paati.

'But you love long hair! You wouldn't let me cut mine last summer because you said it was too beautiful and now you get rid of yours? Not fair, Paati! What's going on?' asked Nandu, feeling annoyed. Not only had her grandmother woken her up in the middle of the night, but she was also rubbing her haircut in Nandu's face.

Paati smiled sympathetically. 'I think you know.'

'No, I don't.'

'Nandu. I realized you were right. That's why I came back. I couldn't leave.'

'Came back? From where?'

Paati smiled encouragingly in the way she always did when Nandu struggled with converting fractions to decimals. It was her 'think, Nandu, think' smile.

'Oh! You! You're a-, y-y-you...are you?' Nandu babbled as realization dawned.

No. This couldn't be happening. Uh-uh. Nandu scrunched her eyes shut.

'Just like when you were a baby, Nandu. You thought that if you closed your eyes everything would be fine.'

'You're a, you're a-'

'Yes, kanna. I'm a ghost.'

In the morning, Nandu stared at her bowl of chocos as though the floating moons and stars were the most fascinating bits of bobbing cereal in the world. She knew that if she looked up, she would have to meet the worried looks of her parents.

She had woken them up with a milk-curdling scream last night and they'd found her hiding beneath her blanket and shaking like a 6.7 magnitude earthquake.

'P-paati!' Nandu had whispered, pointing at the edge of her bed.

'What about Paati?' her mother asked.

'She was sitting right here.'

'Paati? In your room?'

'Yes!'

'Oh, Nandu. Paati died last month. Remember?'

'I remember. I was there. But she was here. I swear. She'd cut her hair! She came to show me!'

Nandu's father smiled sadly. 'Well, that's impossible. You know how much Paati hated short hair. See, it can't have been her. It was just a dream. You miss her, Nandu, we all do. And sometimes the people we miss and love come to us in our dreams. We understand.'

Her mother had stayed with Nandu till she pretended to fall asleep. But once Amma left, Nandu had jumped up and checked for her grandmother under her bed, inside her closets, behind the curtains and even inside the chest of drawers. But she'd found nothing.

Nandu knew the episode had freaked her parents out, because when she came down for breakfast the next morning, they had greeted her with an overt display of fake cheerfulness. The Bhaskars were many things—techies, upma lovers, terrible singers—but they were not morning people. On regular days they refused to communicate via anything other than grunts, snorts and hand gestures till 9 a.m.

'So! How are we feeling this morning?' her mother had trilled, gripping her mug of coffee. 'Any more...umm?'

'Hallucinations?' Nandu offered helpfully.

'I was going to say dreams,' Amma said.

'You're always so dramatic,' said a voice.

Nandu summoned up every millilitre of willpower to not shriek. Her grandmother had sat down next to her with a bowl of chocos.

Her parents were distracted with their phones, her mother attempting Wordle and her father huffing over traffic diversions being made in preparation for a politician's rally.

'She's not here,' Nandu muttered under her breath.

'Now that's rude,' said Paati. 'I raised you with better manners than that. I am very much here and ready to try some of these chocos you love so much.'

Nandu took in a quick and quiet gasp which drew an enquiring look from her mother.

'Gasps!' Nandu said, 'Try Gasps!'

Her mother tapped in the word and smiled. 'A and P are in the right place. Thank you!'

Paati had been a strong believer in hot, freshly made breakfasts and had a deep and abiding mistrust of any food that came out of a cardboard box with a monkey on the front. Most mornings, they would clash over Nandu's breakfast choices.

'Pancake? But dosa is an Indian pancake. Actually, pancakes are foreign dosas. Those people are always stealing our ideas and calling it theirs,' she had snapped when Nandu had once begged for chocolate-chip pancakes. *That* Paati was eating chocos for breakfast? Well, she hadn't eaten them yet, but was sniffing the bowl like a bomb squad canine.

Nandu pushed her half-eaten bowl of chocos away and stood up. 'I'm going to get ready for school,' she said.

'Are you sure you don't want to stay home today?' asked Appa.

Nandu looked at her grandmother who had just spat out the spoon of cereal she'd put into her mouth. 'No, I think I'm better off at school.'

Nandu took the stairs up three at a time and then ran to her bedroom and shut the door behind her, repeating ‘There's no such thing as ghosts. No such thing as ghosts’, out loud as she leaned against her BTS poster.

‘You know, I believe it was Salman Rushdie who said ghosts were about unfinished business,’ said Paati.

Nandu let out a short and shrill scream.

‘Nanduuu!’ Amma called out. ‘Is everything okay?’

‘Fine! It's just a spider!’ she called back.

‘A spider! Ha. I've been called many things in my life, but never that,’ Paati said.

‘You are not here,’ said Nandu firmly.

‘Of course I am. Why would you be speaking to me if I weren't?’ Paati said.

Nandu picked up a cushion and threw it at her grandmother who caught it neatly with both hands.

‘Are you still alive? Have you been pranking us?’ Nandu asked.

‘Pranking?’ Her grandmother sniffed. ‘How distasteful.’

'Then you're a ghost?'

'I suppose you could call me that though I prefer "soulful apparition".'

'You just like using fancy words. Why are you here? Did I do something wrong? Are you going to haunt me forever?' Nandu asked fretfully.

Paati sighed. 'I see you're still jumping to conclusions. I'm not here to haunt you, Nandu. I'm here to know what it's like to be you.'

'Why?' asked Nandu.

'Well, during one of our more...spirited discussions you said that I didn't get you. I'll admit, it took me some time to understand the meaning of the phrase "get me", but when I did, I thought I should rectify this grave mistake (pun intended) and do my best to get you.'

'Did you just use air quotes?' asked Nandu.

'I believe I did. So here I am, ready to do all the things I can to "get" you: experience your deepest wishes and desires, even the ones that I perhaps played a role in denying. Think of it as a kind of bucket list of the afterlife.'

'Nanduuu, ready?' her father called out.

'Five minutes!' Nandu yelled back. 'I have to go to school. Don't do anything while I'm gone, okay?'

'I may be dead but I am still your grandmother. Do not presume to tell me what to do!'

* * *

On the best of days, paying attention in class was a struggle for Nandu, but that morning she didn't even try. She just told every teacher she wasn't feeling well and sat at her desk with her head down on the table. Most of them were fine with it, except for Arlene Ma'am, her Geography teacher, who was convinced that all children were pathological liars.

'You look fine to me!' Ma'am snapped, before dividing the class into groups for map work.

Nandu wasn't sure why they had to know how to mark things on maps when good old Google could just tell you instead. Nandu's group mates Raahil and Janya couldn't agree on where the Aravalli range was.

'Right there,' said an exasperated voice.

Nandu had spent the morning on crimson alert, waiting for her grandmother to jump out at her. When she finally heard her voice, she sagged in relief, glad that the agonizing wait was over. Paati was standing behind Raahil and pointing to a place on the map.

'Don't glare at me!' she said to Nandu. 'I couldn't bear another minute of all your dithering.'

'I told you to stay at home,' said Nandu.

'What?' asked Janya.

'I said the Aravallis are here,' Nandu said, pointing.

'You said it was over here like a minute ago,' said Raahil snottily.

'I was wrong,' said Nandu, marking the range with a series of brown inverted v's on their map.

'What an ill-mannered child,' said Paati. 'Next question, mark the Deccan Plateau. God, is this all they're teaching you these days? And you complain that school's so hard! For this? Move aside, Nandu.'

* * *

The rest of the day was a repeat of Geography with Paati sitting in on every class and answering all the questions loudly and out of turn. Of course, only Nandu could hear her. She identified all the literary devices in a Tagore poem, could correctly name the parts of a shoe flower and even remembered in which year the Battle of Plassey was fought.

'Probably because you were born that year', Nandu snapped sourly at her grandmother who had followed her into the girls' bathroom after lunch.

'Rude,' her grandmother sniffed, 'and untrue.'

'Why are you here Paati?' Nandu yelled.

'Do not raise your voice at me! I told you—'

'Yes, I know. To get to know what it's like to be me. But you haven't done that at all. All you've done is scare me in the middle of the night and then act like a total nerd at school answering all the questions and making it sound like I'm an idiot. Name one thing you did apart from cutting your hair to understand me and what I want.'

Paati looked uncomfortable at this accusation.

'Well...'

'Are you talking to yourself?' a voice asked. It was Priya from D section.

'No,' said Nandu.

'Don't worry. I talk to myself all the time. It helps, doesn't it?' Priya said, smiling serenely as she washed her hands.

After Priya left the loo, Nandu turned to face her grandmother.

'That girl didn't wash her hands properly. Not even for the length of a full happy birthday. Shall I go tell her?' said Paati.

'NO! GO HOME!'

Nandu stomped into the house tired and hungry that afternoon.

'Hello! Anybody there?'

Before she died, Paati had always been there to welcome Nandu home from school while her parents were at work. Now that Paati was gone, Amma and Appa took turns working from home till they could figure out what to do with Nandu after school.

'I'm in here!' her father called from what used to be Paati's room.

‘Hi Appa,’ Nandu said as she walked in.

‘How was school today? Were you okay? All fine?’ Appa asked as he typed something rapidly.

‘You mean did I see any apparitions? Ghostly faces at the window? Nope!’ Nandu lied easily. ‘Is there anything to eat?’

Nandu’s father looked up from his screen with a guilty expression. ‘Bananas? Maybe? Give me a minute? I’ll be done with this and then I’ll make some upma for snacks.’

Nandu sighed and dragged her bag upstairs to her room.

If there was one thing she really, really missed about Paati was having her waiting for Nandu when she came home from school. Always with a smile, a story or some news and an amazing snack: cheese dosas, vadai, paniharam. After they’d washed the snack down with buttermilk or lime juice, Paati would teach Nandu how to play poker and cheat at it, or they’d water the plants together or play word games.

But then Nandu had turned twelve and she hadn’t always felt like doing these things with Paati. She wanted to go hang out with Ameya down the street. Or watch Netflix. Their arguments had started around this time too—over Nandu's desire for a phone, wanting to go to sleepovers and watch movies with her friends alone in the theatre. Paati had thought she was too young for all of these things and had convinced Nandu's parents that she was right.

Nandu opened the door to her room and came to an abrupt halt. Her cupboard doors were wide open and there were piles of clothes and shoes everywhere. She had definitely not left her room like this in the morning.

'Paati?' she asked hesitantly 'Are you in here?'

The bathroom door opened and Paati came out wearing Nandu's favourite jeans and a yellow Star Trek T-shirt.

'Umm. Hello? What's going on?' asked Nandu.

Paati did a twirl and asked, 'What do you think?'

'I'm thinking how did you manage to fit into my jeans!'

Paati smiled cheekily. 'I'm a soulful apparition. I have my ways!'

'Are you going somewhere, Paati?'

'Well after you stormed out of the bathroom today, I thought about what you said and realized you were right: I was showing off at school. And I really hadn't done anything to see what it was like to be you. So I thought why not spend the day walking in Nandu's shoes? Or jeans! Plus, I was tired of wearing that same saree every day over and over again. Do you mind?'

'No! Of course not. So...'

'So?' asked Paati.

'What do you think? You used to hate me wearing these jeans,' Nandu said, pointing to the large tears she'd made at the knees.

'I actually don't mind them.'

'Right?'

'I can't believe I never had a pair.'

'Wait till you try on my joggers. You'll die and go straight to heaven!'

Nandu stopped and clasped her mouth shut with both hands. How could she have been so insensitive? But then Paati started laughing that warm, velvety laugh of hers and Nandu knew it would be alright.

For the next hour Nandu got Paati to try on every item of clothing she owned that her grandmother had once disapproved of. Her Black Pink concert T-shirt. The Demagorgon outfit she'd bought for Halloween, a festival Paati abhorred with all her might. Even her dungarees.

'No more, I'm exhausted,' insisted Paati.

'Wait! You have to try one last thing,' Nandu said, holding out the clothes. Paati looked at the items uncertainly before she took them inside.

'What's taking you so long?' Nandu called out after five minutes.

The bathroom door opened and Paati came out in Nandu's basketball shorts and Argentina Number 10 T-shirt.

'Well?'

'I can see why you hated taking this off. It's so soft and comfortable. I could live in these. Or be dead in these for eternity,' Paati said. Nandu giggled.

'Why did you hate me wearing these then?' Nandu asked.

Paati sat down on the bed next to Nandu and took her hand.

'Well for one thing, you never took them off and they were beginning to smell strange. But, I think I was being a little silly. You were just... growing up too fast for me, and I wanted you to stay a baby a little longer, and...listen to me.'

'But I'm not a baby anymore, Paati. But I'll also always be your baby too. If that makes sense.'

'It actually does,' said Paati, smiling.

'I'm sorry if I was a brat sometimes,' Nandu said, her eyes filling with tears.

'Sometimes?' laughed Paati.

'Okay. More than sometimes,' Nandu agreed. 'I hate that we fought so much that week. Before, you know.'

'I know. I do too,' said Paati.

'Do you remember what we fought about?' asked Nandu.

'I wanted to teach you how to make an omelette. And you wanted to colour some stripes in your hair.'

'Streaks, Paati, streaks. In Viva magenta—the Pantone colour of the year.'

'Whatever!'

'OMG! Did you just say whatever?'

'Maybe,' Paati grinned.

'I think we should settle our fight.'

'How?'

* * *

Nandu slid the prettily plated omelette onto the desk next to her father. He was on a call, but when he saw the plate his eyes lit up and he blew Nandu a kiss.

She went back to the kitchen and sat down to eat her own.

'You were right. This *was* easy and it *is* nice to be able to make something when you're hungry,' she told Paati.

'It is! You know, I didn't want you to learn to cook because you're a girl, Nandu. But because it's a life skill just like swimming or driving,' said Paati.

'Can I learn how to drive next?' asked Nandu, pushing some cheese into her mouth.

'When you're fifty. You can get a phone then too,' said Paati. 'But there's something I can help you with much, much sooner,' Paati said.

'Are you sure this is going to work?' asked Nandu as she watched her grandmother admire herself in the mirror, stroking her hair, which in addition to being short and stylish now had a vivid magenta steak going down one side.

'Well, we won't know unless I try. Since I convinced your mother to not let you stripe your hair when I was alive, the least I can do now is try and convince her to let you do it. Plus, I can't wait to see the look on her face when she sees me!' said Paati yawning.

'Are you okay, Paati? You look tired.'

'I think after tonight it might be time for me to move on.'

'But we haven't watched *Mandalorian* yet! Or listened to Dua Lipa together!'

'I know. I wish we had more time. I'm sorry, Nandu.'

'Will you stay with me till I fall asleep?' asked Nandu.

'Totes!'

'No one says that anymore, Paati.'

* * *

Nalini Bhaskar woke up with a start, and that strange sensation down the back of her neck, the kind you get when you feel like you're not alone. She reached out and switched on her night lamp before slipping her glasses on, sighing with relief as the room came into focus.

At the edge of her bed sat her mother, who for some reason was dressed in basketball shorts, a Messi T-shirt and magenta-coloured hair.

'Hello Nalini! So, I've been thinking, I was wrong about this before and this summer, you should totes let Nandu streak her hair!'

Nandu was woken up by the sound of her mother screaming.

She smiled to herself.

Viva Magenta! Viva Paati!

The Surprise Act

NANDITA DA CUNHA

'The big question is...what will you perform?' asked Mirelle, chewing her braid and watching Grandpa squirm in his chair.

'Who is performing? I don't remember saying I'll come,' he shot back.

'Of course you're coming. *Everyone's* grandparents are coming. So, do you know any magic tricks? Origami? Haikus?'

'You want to make a performing monkey of me?' Grandpa bellowed, lifting his eyebrows and then his newspaper as high as it took to block her out. 'Anyway, I won't be there.'

'Grandpa,' she said sternly, peeping over his paper, 'you've always told me to do my duty. For Grandparents Day, teacher said all grandparents have to come to class, and each gets a turn to perform something. This is your duty.'

But Grandpa only snorted and cast aside his paper in a huffy-puffy way. 'Eh Mimi baby, I don't have the time for this,' he muttered.

Mirelle sighed and looked pointedly at him sprawling in 'The Chair'. From the time he rose, till the time he slept, Grandpa lived in that plush, purple, wingback chair. (Okay, except for when he got himself to the balcony to wave her off to school every morning.) He did sudokus and played Scrabble with her sitting in that chair, watched TV in it, even ate in it. If only he got himself out of it, he'd find all the time in the world, she thought, gritting her teeth. Aloud, she said, 'Ira's Dada-Dadi are coming, Uma has four grandparents and they're all coming.'

'Ah. You, my poor dear have one and he isn't spending his morning in some school with noisy, rowdy...'

'Grandpa!' cried Mirelle, hands on hip, lower lip stuck out, voice getting all squeaky as it did when she got agitated. When that didn't work, she lowered her voice, and fluttered folded hands in his face dramatically, 'Pleeeease? If *you* can't do this, who can?'

'Take your mother,' he said, shooing off her mother, who was dusting breakfast crumbs off him. 'She is good at being a grandmother. And a lecturer. She will do well in a school.'

'What's this, Mirelle?' asked Mama, ignoring Grandpa.

Mirelle read out from the gold-rimmed card in her hand while Grandpa groaned, trying not to look at Mama making big eyes at him from behind Mirelle:

'The 10th, next month is Grandparents Day!

'We'd like to invite you to class, to say

'"Thank you, we love you,

So come on over

Sing, Dance, Perform, Make merry!

With joy and chai and samosas let's—"'

'Samosas!' Suddenly Grandpa sat up, his eyes, brightening. 'You hadn't mentioned samosas.'

'It's settled then,' cooed Mirelle's mother, 'and there's a month to go, plenty of time to decide what you shall perform.'

Grandpa sat back. 'I'll come on one condition—NO performance,' and he shut his eyes.

Mirelle decided to continue the conversation later. Winning one battle was victory enough for one morning.

Later, at school lunch break with Ira and Uma, she realized the battle had just begun.

'My Dadi is telling a story. In five languages. Like she does in her podcast? *Dadi ki Kahaani*?'

'My grandad is in Singapore. So he will join on Zoom and make a presentation on "The role of grandparents in modern times".'

Saved by the class bell, Mirelle felt a ringing in her head that wouldn't go away. 'Come on, Grandpa,' she thought, 'there must be something you can do.' The headache and worrying continued all day and when she got back, she threw herself on her bed in despair. The trophies atop her cupboards looked down at her. 'Bandra Zonals Elocution. First place', 'Interschool chess. Runner up', 'Primary School debating champ'. Was there anything she wasn't the best at? 'Producing a grandparent who could perform,' mocked the ringing voice in her head. She stomped out and woke Grandpa from his late afternoon siesta.

'Have you thought about what you're going to perform?' she demanded.

'Ungh,' grunted Grandpa, eyes falling shut again.

'What will Ira think? What will Noorie say?' her voice rose higher. But he'd resumed snoring.

'You're lucky he's turning up,' said her mother. 'When I was your age, he was at his clinic or the hospital from before I woke up, until well after I'd slept off.'

Mirelle made a sound, suspiciously like *Ungh*. Grandpa may have been a big, famous orthopedic surgeon but what use was that right now? If he'd been a pilot, he could talk of his travels. If he'd been a scientist, he could wow her friends with experiments. But it's not like any of them were in need of a hip replacement or urgent spinal work. 'Looks like he is more than making up now,' she cried, dragging her feet out. 'Looks like he is going to sit superglued to that chair forever!'

Grandpa opened an eye after she'd left.

'Recite a poem?' suggested her mother. 'You used to read poetry.'

'Used to,' said Grandpa. 'And how will I remember the lines now?'

'Your old puppet act?'

He held up his hand, showing his now quivering fingers.

'Sing your Elvis medley?'

'Tchah. Can't do the steps anymore. No point without it.'

'The point is that Mirelle appears quite bothered about this,' sighed Mama.

She'd assumed he'd fallen back asleep, so was startled several minutes later to hear: 'I could call Glen. He may have one of his bright ideas.'

Grandpa hadn't stirred to call his brother in weeks, so Mama rushed to get the phone before he changed his mind. A plan got fixed. Glen would meet him at the club the next morning, and over breakfast and bridge (Glen's bridge card group played every Tuesday) he would get his advice.

But Tuesday didn't work out like either Grandpa or Mirelle would have liked. Grandpa did meet Glen and his gang. Over egg bhurjee, filter coffee and masala cheese toast (Mama wasn't around to make big eyes), the morning raced by, as they argued amicably over different topics from politicians to footballers to stock prices. But when it came to performing for a fifth grader's class, the gang's ideas were too outlandish (juggle eggs?) or too outdated (grab a kerchief and dance a *mando*?) or too *not* Grandpa (clowning!). The only decision taken was that Grandpa would join Glen and the gang every Tuesday to play bridge.

Meanwhile at school, Mirelle's stomach flipped to hear Ira suggest: 'Miss, shall we have prizes for best grandparent performances?' 'Nooo,' she heard herself call out, 'I mean, it shouldn't be a competition. It's about *participating*, and sharing talents.' She didn't look the way of her puzzled friends. This wasn't the Mirelle they knew, who welcomed the idea of any competition (which she inevitably won) with glittering eyes! What was up?

She came home so gloomy, she didn't notice the equally gloomy look on Grandpa's face. Grandpa had another idea after Mirelle went to sleep that night. 'My old assistant doctor,

Anjali? She will understand this stuff, she used to organize our events, and has two young girls. I'll speak to her.' Mama rushed in with the phone and Anjali's number was promptly dialled.

'Dr Almeida! I didn't realize you're still...err... umm...active.'

'Heh! Who told you otherwise? Anyway, I wanted your advice.'

'Then why not join me at our Free Orthopedic Health Camp for deserving patients tomorrow? We could do with your consultation skills.'

That Saturday, Anjali's camp had queues that extended till the gates of Holy Family Hospital and beyond. Grandpa was rushed off his feet. Later, he caught hold of his old assistant and shared his new problem. Anjali had several ideas and he wrote them down gratefully. He marched home with the list (and with not just a little pride in the fact that he had apparently *not* forgotten old skills. His work at the camp had been much appreciated and somehow, he'd agreed to drop in every Saturday to help out).

Sadly, Mama pooh-poohed the list even before he could share it with Mirelle. 'The

Caterpillar book? Bubble tricks? Animal game? How old are Anjali's kids? Three?'

'Err...two and four,' Grandpa admitted.

'This won't do for fifth graders. Keep thinking!'

As a last resort, that Sunday, Grandpa met up with his old school chum Eddie, who dragged him for a walk down the Bandra seafront promenade. But...

'Performance ideas? You were always the ideas man. I just said yes-yes, let me help, so I could meet you,' chuckled Eddie. 'It's been ten years! Or is it fifteen? When did you retire?'

Grandpa was enjoying his morning walk too much to be annoyed by this deception. The 'ten, or was it fifteen?' years melted away as the old friends munched roasted sing-dana and watched the world go by that windy morning. Eddie even extracted a promise from Grandpa that he'd join him every Sunday.

Suddenly, Grandpa's days became hectic what with Bridge Tuesdays, Health Camp Saturdays and Walking Sundays... Mama and Mirelle watched open-mouthed, as he got up, got dressed and left the house before one could say 'Purple Wingback Chair'. Yet Mirelle's days grew increasingly harassed. Grandpa didn't remotely have a performance plan in sight. If she brought up the topic, he'd roar: 'What is this what will Noorie say, what will Poori think? Who cares?' He clearly didn't. Her suspicious friends regularly pestered her about what he was going to do.

One hot, sticky day, Noorie whispered from the next desk:

'Why aren't you telling what your grandfather will perform?'

'Why must you know everything?'

'Is it lame? That's why you didn't want prizes?'

'Noorie! No!'

'Then why?'

'Why why... Because the sky is so high.'

'He hasn't told you? Or...'

'Okay. It's a SURPRISE act.'

'Ohh. What kind of surprise?'

'The kind that will make your eyes go round as poories.'

From then on, word spread. The mystery around Mirelle's Grandpa's surprise act grew... It would make your nose quiver like jelly, your mouth stretch wide as a roomali roti, it would freeze your brain, squeeze your knees, it promised a sight unlike any. Through this, Mirelle grew more and more silent and aloof. But her shrugs and disinterested *unghs*, only fuelled the excited rumours. This was not going to end well.

Grandpa and Mama watched her drag herself about. Mama noticed, with surprise, that Grandpa seemed strangely unaffected. Mirelle didn't notice anything. Her mind had turned to damage control. What excuse could she make? How about: 'We didn't want to upstage anyone, so I told him not to do anything.' Or: 'Performers need viewers, na? So Grandpa decided just to watch. So noble, na?' But coming from *her*, this would be tough to swallow. Should she go without him? Would Grandpa mind? It's not like he was thrilled to go at first. She'd be doing him a favour. With everyone's expectations about his performance, he was going to fall flat on his face (and take her down with him).

The night before the event, her insides felt churny and her mouth had turned sour. At school, all anyone talked about was, 'What was Cool Mirelle's Cool Grandpa going to perform?' Why had she opened her mouth to Noorie? Why? Anger bubbled inside her. This was Grandpa's fault for refusing to be a sport. She decided to call it off and headed to his room. The light was on as he was still awake. 'Grandpa?' she called out. He opened the door...glowing, excited. His bed was strewn with clothes.

He held up two shirts. 'Which one for tomorrow, eh Mimi? A suit might be too hot.'

'The grey one,' she muttered and fled. Too late.

She woke up to a dull and dreary day.

'Happy Grandparents Day, Grandpa,' Mirelle muttered at breakfast.

Later, her classmates chorused—'Happy Grandparents Day, Grandparents,' as they entered their classroom arms linked with grandparents.

After a tour of the classroom, everyone sat down for the performances. Mirelle froze. The programme was chalked out on the blackboard. The last act was: 'Dr Leo Almeida: Surprise Act.' Her teacher had heard the rumour too! What was Mirelle going to do? What would Grandpa do? Sneaking a glance, she saw he was in the same upbeat mood he'd been in all morning, smiling around. Everyone smiled back at him, many stared in open curiosity...she knew what they were curious about.

The performances began. With each act, the cheers grew louder, but the ringing inside her head drowned them out. Her face went hot and her hands got clammy.

'Grandpa,' she whispered. He was enjoying himself, humming along to one grandparent's melodious Kishore Kumar medley, tapping along to another's expert drumming set. Soon it was time for the final performance.

'Grandpa,' she hissed louder. No response. When she turned, he wasn't by her side. Mouth open, she saw him walking towards the front of the class to frenzied claps. What was going on? She shouldn't have come. She held her head in her hands and looked down, too nervous to meet anyone's eye. Grandpa's voice carried over, loud and clear.

'Good morning! One month ago, I was stumped when my granddaughter Mirelle informed me that I would have to perform at a Grandparents event. I don't sing, I can't dance...'

She heard titters. Her humiliation had begun. She wished she could sink into the ground and disappear. She blinked hard, willing back the tears. But Grandpa was charging on.

'These days I prefer...what do you call it... "chilling" in my chair. But when my Mimi asked me, was I going to sit superglued to my chair to the end? UNGH!' Grandpa shuddered and paused. 'I woke up! I began to get out again. To meet people. Old haunts, new habits. And I decided exactly what I wanted to share today.'

What was this? She was so worried, she was one of the last in the class to notice: One by one, the grandparents were walking up to join Grandpa. They all held small cardboard placards.

At a nod from Grandpa, they turned around the placards and held them up, revealing messages.

'We're here to thank you too! For the times we learn from *you*,' boomed Grandpa. She read the messages.

'Thank you for teaching me to laugh again.' (Ira's Dadi)

'For unearthing my violin for our Sunday Karaoke.' (Ahalya's Paati)

'For leading me to Wordle.' (Seema's Aaji)

'For getting me to research our family tree.' (Noorie's Nani)

'For introducing me to K-Pop.' (Siya's Grandpa)

'For finding my old friends online.' (Noorie's Nana)

'For teaching us this Zoom thing!' (Uma's grandparents nodding away on the screen.)

And on Grandpa's: 'For reminding me to live.'

'Awww,' went everyone. 'Sooper-dooper!' Noorie cried.

Grandpa organized all this? She heard teacher gushing, 'Remarkable... Reached out to me for contacts... Then spoke to each and every grandparent...' Wow. How? So many questions for later. For now Mirelle managed to shrug in her cool way, 'Yeah, yeah, told you all. Whose Grandpa is he any way...' But her eyes went a bit misty, her cheeks pink.

The music was blaring now, and the grandparents began boogeying. Grandpa was surrounded by adoring kids and grandparents. He caught her eye and winked. There were samosa crumbs all over his nice shirt. Sheesh!... Messy... What would Ira's Dadi think? What would... Wait. 'Who cares!' roared a voice in her head.

Letting out a long, deep breath, Mirelle looked at Grandpa and winked back.

When Granny Died

JERRY PINTO

We prayed, Sue and I, we prayed but Granny died anyway. I didn't understand. Aunt Lou said, 'God listens to the prayers of little children.' Now, I'm twelve so I'm not a little child any more. But Sue is four, she counts. She's really little, so why didn't God answer her prayers? We did everything the doctor said we should do. We gave her the pills, she had the operation, she had another operation, Ma sold her gold chain and got a pretty set of beads to wear instead, we let Granny rest, we gave her fruit, we tried to be quiet but she died anyway.

I DON'T WANT TO WRITE THIS.

I HATE WRITING ABOUT THIS.

I START CRYING.

I DON'T LIKE CRYING.

Okay, crying over.

Now I can write again. Dr Mary Ann says crying is good, it's okay to cry. She says it cleans you up inside. It does feel a little better for a while. Like the tank is empty. But then it fills up again. Now while my tear-tank is empty, I can say this.

I loved Granny but I didn't like her. She was mean to Ma but she was good to me. So it made me feel bad when she was nice to me after being mean to Ma. And she was good to me but not so good with Sue. She gave me a chocolate bar for my birthday but she gave Sue an éclair for hers. 'You're a boy, you need more,' she would say.

Now she's gone.

I'M CRYING AGAIN.

WAIT.

I'LL BE BACK.

Shee, I had to blow my nose that time. No, I want to tell you about Granny. She could embroider all kinds of things. She could make great pickle. We still have a jar of her brinjal pickle. I open it sometimes because its smell reminds me of her. She loved WWF and she would watch it with me and she would shout 'Aavois!' when one of the wrestlers threw another. Every Wednesday she went to the novena at Mahim Church and she would almost cause a riot because she would take a big bag of Kismi toffees with her and give to all the street kids. Sometimes they would grab at the bag and she would mutter angrily, 'Suffer not the little children to come unto me.' They would calm down and back off a little because my Granny muttering was like acid rain. You had to jump out of the way.

I asked Grandpa once: How can you love her?

And he said: 'People are not buffets. You don't get to choose the nice bits. You get the whole person.'

So I tried.

But she's gone.

BUT THESE TEARS KEEP COMING BACK.

WHETHER YOU WANT THEM OR NOT.

TWO MINUTES, GIVE ME TWO MINUTES.

One day, Grandpa found me crying over *The Book of Stars* by Terry Gomes. I love astronomy. I got a big book from Ma for my eighth birthday before Granny fell ill. It is a beautiful book and tells you how the stars know the whole story, from the beginning of time. And how you can even hear some of the Big Bang in the sky right now if you have the right ears. But the book is old now and it doesn't have the latest pictures from the James Webb telescope. Someone told me a new edition had come out. I checked it on the Net and it costs a lot of money so I didn't tell anyone I wanted it but Grandpa must have seen me looking at it so he said we should make our own book. We cut out whatever comes in the papers or magazines from Hubble or Cassini's pictures of Saturn and we stick them in. And once a week, I am allowed to choose one picture to download and print out at Mayur Stationery so that's cool.

Most of the time, looking at my book calms me but this time it didn't work and I was crying, so Grandpa sat near me. He put his arm across my shoulders and I waited but he didn't say anything. Granny was a big one for telling her mind. Grandpa is a big one for not saying anything. When everyone is angry and shouting, he just listens. He loves reading and right now he is reading *Living with Death and Dying* by Elizabeth Kubler-Ross with two dots on the 'u' in Kubler. I like those dots—they look like eyes looking out for u. I asked him if I should read the book and he smiled and said, 'Soon.'

Grandpa likes to answer like that. Or else he doesn't answer at all. He doesn't nod or shake his head or smile or anything. He just listens quietly, not saying 'yes' and not saying 'no'. He just listens. And generally people calm down and say things like, 'I'm not saying that she's a bad person...' and 'Okay, maybe I am overreacting...' That's when Grandpa has his say.

So maybe crying is like shouting? Maybe when you're crying, you're not listening? Maybe Grandpa was waiting for me to stop crying so he could start talking.

'It's okay,' I said when I could talk. 'I'm fine.'

He chuckled.

'Yes, everyone cries when they're fine!'

I managed a watery smile because it was not just a Dad joke, it was a Granddad joke.

'Let me tell you where Granny began...'

'I know. She was born in Moira...'

'No, even before that. In the beginning there was everything but it was all packed into a tiny, tiny space. Then it all burst open...'

‘Grandpa, I know the Big Bang Theory.’

‘Oh yes, but the great mystery is why there is anything at all. When this happened, every plus should have cancelled every minus and the result should have been zero. But that didn’t happen. Instead, something did come out of that huge explosion. And not just something but so much: stars and planets and meteors and asteroids and pulsars and quasars...on the big level. And then came life and plants and fish and animals and people and Grandma!’

‘I know all that.’

‘So at some point the stars want us back. That’s when we die and slowly we become stardust again. Tonight, we’ll go up on the terrace and we’ll look for Granny.’

‘I’ll come too,’ said Sue who had wandered up. She’s at that age where she wants to go everywhere.

‘Sure,’ said Grandpa. ‘We’ll all go.’

* * *

So that night Ma packed sandwiches and apples and milkshakes and we went up to the terrace. We threw chatais down and Ma and Daddy went for a walk around the edge of the terrace but Grandpa and Sue and I lay down and looked up.

Sue said: 'What happened to Granny?'

'She's a pulsar,' I said.

Grandpa laughed.

'Sue, do you remember how we found a caterpillar and we put it in a bowl with some leaves? And how it ate and ate and then rolled up into a ball and then became a butterfly?'

'Yes,' said Sue. She had wanted to keep the butterfly as a pet but Grandpa had said it would be happy in a garden and so we went to the park in the zoo and let it go there and then Grandpa took her to see the penguins so she stopped crying after a while.

'Granny has become a butterfly. She pushed her way out of her body and now she's dancing on the tops of flowers...'

And then a big moth fluttered down and bumped into Grandpa's bald head before flying away.

'I think Grandma has come a moth,' said Sue.

I'M GOING TO CRY AGAIN.

NO...I'M GOING TO LAUGH.

OH...OH...I'M LAUGHING AND CRYING AT THE SAME TIME.

Contributors

When **Adithi Rao** is not gobbling chocolate, she writes books, short stories, plays and the occasional film script. She is part-time faculty at the Srishti Manipal Institute of Art, Design & Technology, and full-time mom to six street dogs and one little human. You can find her on www.adithirao.com.

Andaleeb Wajid is a hybrid author, having published forty novels in the past fourteen years. Andaleeb enjoys writing in a number of different genres such as young adult, romance, and horror. Andaleeb's romance trilogy, the Jasmine Villa Series, was published by Westland in February 2023. She has an upcoming YA horror novel with HarperCollins later in 2023.

Ashok Banker began writing stories at the age of nine. He has been unable to stop since then.

Please send help—and biscuits, lots of biscuits. Check out his funny-spooky series *The Secret School Mysteries: The Invisible Spy*, *Aliens Ate My Homework*, *The Haunted Centre*.

Ashok Rajagopalan is a writer and illustrator of children's books. He mostly writes funny stories and draws pictures. He lives with his family and books in a quiet part of Chennai. He thinks that grandparents are the best people in the world and hopes to become one soon.

When **Bijal Vachharajani** is not reading a children's book, she's writing or editing one. Her planet-friendly books include *A Cloud Called Bhura*, which won the Auther prize in 2020. She is a certified climate worrier.

Deepa Agarwal is the author of over sixty books for children and adults. Several of her books have received awards. Her greatest award, however, is the presence of five adorable grandchildren in her life. They have been a wonderful adventure and a great learning experience too. She continues to receive enlightenment in their company.

Harshikaa's nani was full of stories—of her childhood, of a young girl married into a large house, of Partition. She had had her losses and her moments of grief and of resilience as she set up home in a small room in Mumbai. She made sure her children and her grandchildren saw each of those emotions, and Harshikaa brings a bit of her into whatever she writes.

Jerry Pinto was born when only his maternal grandmother was alive. His grandfathers died before him. He wants you to know that he has been worried about dying for a long time and so he was reading Elizabeth Kübler-Ross's book while he was writing this story. Dr Ross thought a lot about dying and about how people faced it and she used the two metaphors of stardust and butterflies that he has used in this story. Thanks, Dr Ross!

Menaka Raman is the author of a number of books for children including *Topi Rockets from Thumba*, *Loki Takes Guard* and *The Great Escape*. *Loki Takes Guard* won the Valley of Words Award for Writing for Young Adults. Her short stories have appeared in anthologies published by Penguin, Speaking Tiger, and Scholastic India. She has written parenting and children's books for some of India's leading newspapers and magazines including *The New Indian Express*, *The Hindu Sunday Magazine* and *Vogue* India.

Nandini Nayar is the award-winning author of over sixty books for children. *What Shall I Make*? was named an outstanding book by the USSBBY while *Sometimes Mama, Sometimes Papa* and *Mini's Questions*, are on the Parag Honour List. For more information, please visit www.nandininayar.in.

Nandita da Cunha is an award-winning children's book author based in Mumbai. After her MBA at XLRI, she worked as a strategy consultant with Arthur Andersen and KPMG before moving on to what makes her happiest—writing for children. Since 2020, she has released eight books, that have received widespread acclaim (featuring on the Parag Honour Lists 2021 and 2023; winning the Neev Book Award, and the FICCI Publishing

Special Jury award). She loves books, her piano, gardening, birdwatching and chocolate—not necessarily in that order!

Ruskin Bond is the author of numerous novellas, short-story collections and non-fiction books, many of them classics. Among them are *When I Was a Boy*, *Lone Fox Dancing*, *The Room on the Roof*, *A Flight of Pigeons*, and *A Book of Simple Living*. He received the Sahitya Akademi Award in 1993, the Padma Shri in 1999 and the Padma Bhushan in 2014.

Sayantan Ghosh lives in New Delhi, and is executive editor at Simon & Schuster India. His work has been published in *Ambit Magazine*, *Electric Literature*, *Litro Magazine*, *Firstpost*, *The Telegraph*, *National Herald*, *The Hindu Business Line*, *News9*, and *The Times of India*, among others, and he writes a weekly book recommendation column for *DailyO*. He was shortlisted for the Editor of the Year award at the Publishing Next Industry Awards 2021.

Swapna Dutta, with around fifty titles to her credit, including translations, has been published by Hachette, Scholastic, National Book Trust, Orient Blackswan, Srishti and Ukiyoto, among others. She has contributed to dailies like *Deccan Herald*, *The Hindu*, *The Times of India*, *Hindustan Times*, *Indian Express*, *Pioneer*, *Asian Age*, and *The Telegraph* and magazines like *Indian Literature*, *The Little Magazine*, *Scottish Home & Country* (UK), *The School Magazine* (Australia), *The Bookbird* (USA), among others. She worked for Living Media, Limca Book of Records; and Encyclopaedia Britannica between 1988 and 2002.

Varsha Seshan is a writer of lists, emails, and notes to herself. She also writes children's stories, and loves windy, rainy days, full of magic and possibility. She conducts online book clubs and writing programmes for ages seven to fourteen. Find out more at www.varshaseshan.com